CHILDREN'S CONCISE GEOGRAPHY ENCYCLOPEDIA

General Editor: Michael March
House Editor: Brenda Apsley
Consultant: Gustav Dobrzynski, University of Salford
Art Direction: Bob Swan
Design and Layout: Tony Truscott
Typesetting: Tony Truscott Designs
Index: Ian Horn

Artists
Oxford Illustrators Limited

Copyright © 1993 World International Publishing Limited.
Published in Great Britain by World International Publishing Limited,
An Egmont Company, Egmont House, PO Box 111,
Great Ducie Street, Manchester M60 3BL.

ISBN 0-7498-0844-6

Printed in Spain

World Horizons is an imprint of World International Publishing Limited.

A catalogue record for this book is available from the British Library

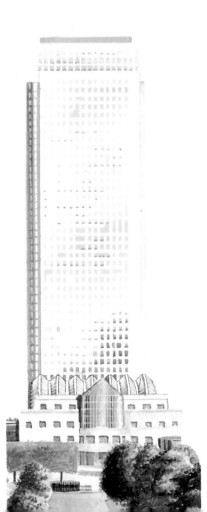

World
HORIZONS

CHILDREN'S
CONCISE
GEOGRAPHY
ENCYCLOPEDIA

JOHN PORTER

Contents

Population

People and Homes

People at Work

Leisure, Travel and Trade

Introduction

Geography is the study of the Earth's surface, of the places on it, and of how people live on the Earth and use it. Geography is concerned with how naturally occurring substances such as plants, minerals and water are used as resources for farming or industry, and how natural features such as lakes or rivers can be made into sources of energy. It distinguishes those parts of the Earth's surface where people and economic activity have become highly concentrated from those where mankind is still largely absent. It looks at how these high concentrations of people and commerce are linked together by roads, railways, airlines or telecommunications.

This encyclopedia looks at all these topics and shows how they are related to each other. Besides explaining them in general terms, it often picks out particular places or instances for detailed illustration. This book includes many maps, for geographers believe that knowledge about the world is not very useful unless we know where places are. Some of the places studied in detail are parts of entire continents, while others are no larger than villages. They have all been chosen to show that the Earth is a very varied place.

Modern science has given geographers the opportunity to study these patterns as never before. Satellites can take pictures of the whole Earth, or can zoom in for detailed views of any part of the Earth's surface. Computers can now assemble enormous amounts of information about the weather, and can make predictions about how much rain farmers might expect to have in ten years' time.

Geographical knowledge becomes increasingly important as the globe seems to 'shrink' around us. Modern communications mean that we can speak to people on the other side of the world in seconds and be with them in hours. Almost all countries are now so bound up with each other in global networks of commerce and finance that events or developments in one country may quickly produce problems for others. In this 'global village' we must all have a sound knowledge of what the rest of the world is like if we are to live and trade with other peoples without conflict.

Most scientists are now agreed that population and economic growth threaten the Earth and its people with disaster, possibly destruction. Geographers are concerned with the great environmental problems of our time such as pollution and global warming. But they also recognize that there are no simple solutions to these developments, and urge people to examine the issues and problems which decisions about the environment can often bring.

To find out the subjects in each of the main sections of this encyclopedia, you can look at the Contents. At the end of each section you will find a page of references, which contains difficult words and ideas not explained in the main text. If you want to find out a particular fact, the place to look is in the Index, which gives the numbers of all relevant pages.

The Earth

The Earth in Space

The Earth is one of the nine planets of our solar system, which has the Sun as its centre. The planets and various moons, comets, dust particles and gases all revolve around the Sun. At a distance of 150 million kilometres (94 million miles) from the Sun, the Earth is the third closest planet (after Mercury and Venus). It is also one of the smaller planets, with a diameter of 12,756km (7,928 miles) compared with 142,800km (88,750 miles) for Jupiter (the largest).

The seasons

The Earth revolves around the Sun in 365.25 days – a whole year. Its axis is tilted at an angle of 66.5 degrees (written 66.5°) to its plane of orbit and always points into space in the same direction. Encircling the Earth at right angles to its axis

The position and movement of the Earth in relation to the Sun determines the seasons and the length of day and night.

is the equator, an imaginary line that divides the Earth into northern and southern hemispheres (meaning 'half spheres').

The tilting of the Earth's axis is responsible for the seasons. In June the northern hemisphere is closer to the Sun than the southern hemisphere, and is therefore warmer. At noon on 21 June – the northern 'summer solstice' –

the Sun is directly above the tropic of Cancer. This is the longest day in the northern hemisphere, when the regions north of the Arctic Circle have 24 hours of continuous daylight.

In December the southern hemisphere is tilted towards the Sun. On 21 December – the southern summer solstice – the southern hemisphere has its longest day and the northern hemisphere its shortest. The Sun is then directly overhead at noon along the tropic of Capricorn and there is continuous daylight south of the Antarctic Circle.

Twice during the year – on 21 March and 21 September – the Sun is overhead at the equator and there day and night are of equal length. These occasions are called the equinoxes (meaning 'equal nights').

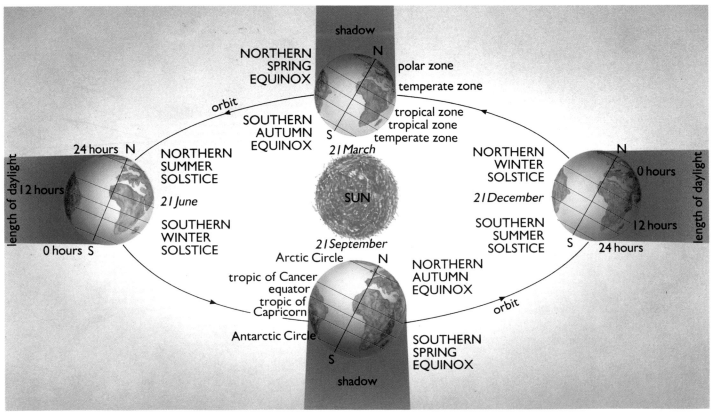

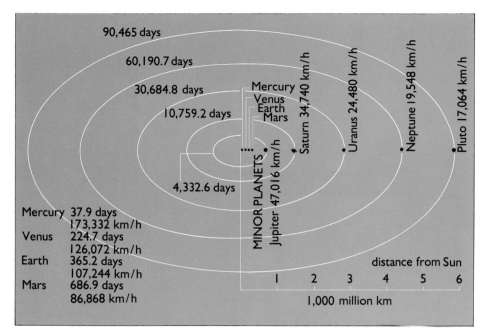

				distance from Sun		
	1	2	3	4	5	6

1,000 million km

90,465 days
60,190.7 days
30,684.8 days
10,759.2 days
4,332.6 days

Mercury
Venus
Earth
Mars

MINOR PLANETS

Jupiter 47,016 km/h
Saturn 34,740 km/h
Uranus 24,480 km/h
Neptune 19,548 km/h
Pluto 17,064 km/h

Mercury 37.9 days
         173,332 km/h
Venus   224.7 days
         126,072 km/h
Earth   365.2 days
         107,244 km/h
Mars   686.9 days
         86,868 km/h

The Earth within the solar system.

The unique planet

The Earth is unlike any other planet in the solar system – and possibly in the universe – in that its atmosphere can support life. Moreover life on Earth continually creates the conditions needed for its own survival. Scientists call this the 'Gaia' theory.

All life-forms on Earth are closely linked together and depend on each other. Heat and water help to sustain life, while the atmosphere blocks out harmful radiation and shields the planet from showers of cosmic particles from outer space.

The atmosphere also provides the temperature and moisture conditions that allow green plants to grow. Plants use the Sun's energy to build their tissues, and these, in turn, convert carbon dioxide from the atmosphere into the oxygen that is needed for other life-forms to develop.

Unwanted heat from the Sun is reflected back into space from light-coloured surfaces. This helps to maintain the Earth at a fairly constant temperature.

The Earth is a huge system for supporting life. The oceans and atmosphere help to circulate nutrients and energy around the planet.

The shadow of human interference

Many people are now worried that human activity is disrupting the system of life on Earth. They point to changes such as the poisoning of the atmosphere by carbon dioxide emitted from factories and motor vehicles. They warn against 'global warming' brought about by the 'greenhouse' effect, when heat is trapped inside the atmosphere. Another danger is the possible destruction of the atmosphere's ozone layer by manufactured gases. This would reduce the effectiveness of the atmosphere to protect us from harmful radiation. There is a growing fear that unless human activities are controlled, they could eventually destroy the whole of life itself.

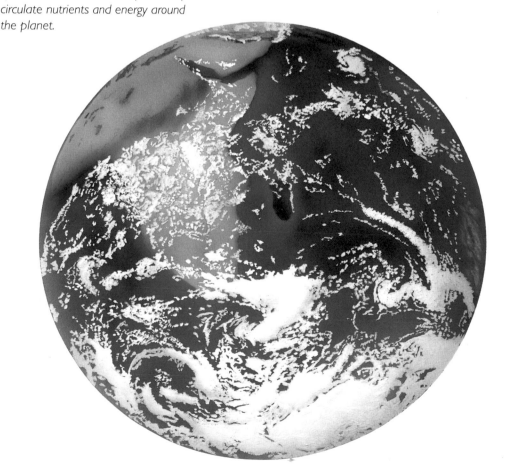

The Earth's Time-Scale

Until modern times people had little idea of the true age of the Earth and its rocks. It was once calculated, from information in the Bible, that the Earth was created in 4004 BC. However, scientists in the 19th century, using geological dating methods, found that it was very much older than this. The first human beings appeared some 2.5 million years ago – a time-span that it is difficult to imagine. Yet this is not very long ago compared with the time when dinosaurs roamed the Earth (100 million years ago), and both these events are very recent when compared with the age of the Earth itself, about 4,500 million years.

An Earth clock

The Earth's time-scale can be compared to a clock which begins to tick at 11.15 pm, with the present being midnight. On this clock all the rocks formed before 11.54 pm would be too old to be properly dated, even with modern scientific methods. Dinosaurs existed about one minute before midnight.

Humankind, in its earliest form, did not appear until one and a half seconds before the midnight stroke.

The earliest rocks are reckoned to be between four and six billion years old. Geologists, scientists who study rocks and their history, use the natural process of 'radioactive decay' to date rocks. This means that, over time, the isotopes of certain elements present in rocks break down ('decay') because they are radioactive and unstable. The 'decay' begins as soon as the new rocks are formed and occurs at a rate that varies according to the isotope. By measuring the amount of radioactive material left in the rock and comparing this with the rate of decay, the geologist can work out how long ago the decay started, and therefore the age of the rock. Rocks up to 100,000 years old can be dated using radiocarbon dating, which makes use of the rate of decay of the isotope carbon-14, captured by rocks and present in the bodies of living things.

Geological time

Geologists divide the last 600 million years of the Earth's history into eras, and eras into periods. The boundaries between the eras are marked by phases of orogeny (mountain building) when the world's great mountain ranges were formed. The most recent of these was the Alpine phase, which produced the European Alps, the Himalayas, and mountains in the South American Andes and the North American Rockies.

Much of the world's landscape is the product of quite recent changes to the Earth's surface. In the northern hemisphere the Ice Ages began 1.5 million years ago, covering much of the northern continents in vast ice sheets and glaciers. The work of the ice sculpted these continents

The Earth's history squeezed into 45 minutes.

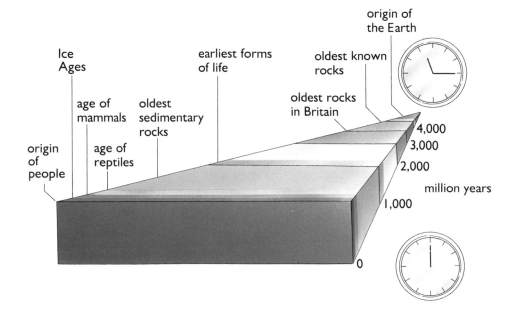

into new shapes, producing much of their present relief. The ice came and went in phases, each of several thousand years, with warmer periods in between. Some scientists think that we are still in one of these warmer spells, and that one day, perhaps long after humankind has disappeared from the Earth, the ice sheets will return.

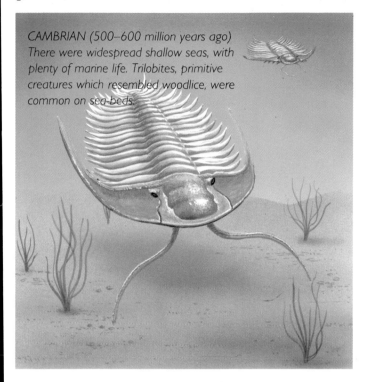

CAMBRIAN (500–600 million years ago)
There were widespread shallow seas, with plenty of marine life. Trilobites, primitive creatures which resembled woodlice, were common on sea-beds.

PERMIAN (225–275 million years ago)
Much of the Earth's surface was desert. Land reptiles and modern insects began to evolve.

JURASSIC (140–175 million years ago)
This was a time of great volcanic activity. Dinosaurs reigned supreme, together with flying reptiles. The first flowering plants appeared among the swamps.

PLEISTOCENE (10,00–1 million years ago)
Great ice sheets covered the northern continents, turning most of the land into a frozen waste. When the ice sheets retreated, mammals increased in number and human beings eventually evolved to dominate the Earth.

The Earth's Structure

The Earth is made up of a number of layers. The core or innermost layer consists of heavy molten metals, mostly iron or nickel, at temperatures of up to 5,000°C. Outside the core is the mantle, a zone of iron and magnesium compounds at about 1,600°C, much of it in a semi-molten state. The crust, or outside layer, is very thin by comparison and forms a skin on top of these inner layers.

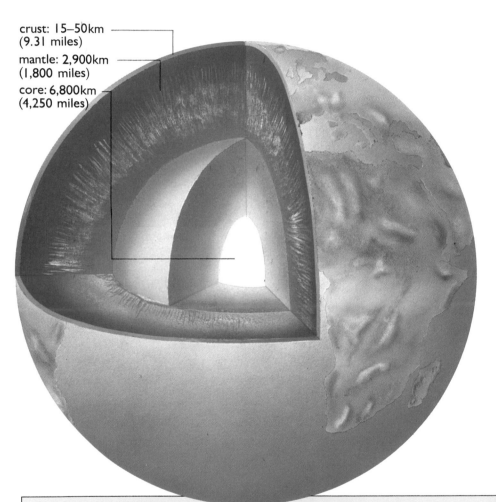

crust: 15–50km (9.31 miles)
mantle: 2,900km (1,800 miles)
core: 6,800km (4,250 miles)

The crust and its behaviour

The Earth's crust is itself composed of layers. The sial, or outer layer, forms the main continental land masses, which are mostly granite. The continents rest on a heavier layer made of sima, or basaltic rock, which extends beneath them and also forms the ocean floors. The continents are like rafts, 'floating' on the heavy sima below them. As well as being made up of layers, the crust is not one single piece across but is divided into a number of sections, called plates.

In some ways the crust behaves more like plastic than solid rock in that lengths of it may bend, twist or fold under pressure. Strains and stresses from within the Earth can fold layers of rock upwards or downwards. Sometimes the layers can be so crumpled that they form new mountain ranges. In other cases the rocks cannot take the strains put upon them and they fracture along lines called faults. Some

Left: *The crust is only the outermost of the layers that make up the structure of the Earth.*

Below: *Basic facts and figures about the Earth.*

THE EARTH'S SURFACE

Highest point on the Earth's surface: Mt Everest, Tibet–Nepal boundary. 8,848m (29,028ft)
Lowest point on the Earth's surface: The Dead Sea, Jordan. Below sea-level 395m (1,296ft)
Greatest ocean depth: Challenger Deep, Marianas. Trench 11,022m (36,161ft)
Average height of land: 840m (2,756ft)
Average depth of seas and oceans 3,808m (12,493ft)

DIMENSIONS

Area of surface: 510 million km²
Land surface: 149 million km²
Land surface as % of total area: 29.2%
Water surface: 361 million km²
Water surface as % of total area: 70.8%
Equatorial circumference: 40,077 km²
Volume of the Earth: 1,083, 230 × 10⁶ km³
Mass of the Earth: 5.9 × 10²¹ tonnes

folds or faults occur over small areas, but others affect the shape of entire continents. Geologists learn much about the history of the Earth from studying the faults and folds in rocks.

Folding and faulting have been going on ever since the Earth was formed. The formation of the Earth's main features takes place so slowly that people are unlikely to notice many changes within their lifetimes. But change is still taking place and will continue for many millions of years to come.

Mountains, plateaux, oceans

The world's highest mountain ranges are known as fold mountains, because they were formed by the folding or crumpling of parts of the crust. The Himalayas, which include Mount Everest (8,848m; 29,028ft), the world's highest mountain, are an example. Other areas of the continents – such as the Mato Grosso of Brazil, the Deccan of India, and most of Tibet – form relatively level raised plateaux.

Along the eastern side of Africa much of the continent has sunk into a deep trench, or rift valley, which stretches for over 5,000km (3,000 miles) from Mozambique to Syria. It includes Lake Malawi, Lake Tanganyika, the Red Sea and the Dead Sea. The shoreline of the Dead Sea is the world's lowest point on land, 393m (1,300ft) below sea-level.

Beneath the oceans are entire systems of underwater mountains and trenches. The deepest of these trenches lie around the edges of the Pacific Basin, where they plunge to depths of 11,000m (36,000ft) below sea-level – much more than some of the world's highest mountain peaks extend upwards. Many of the trenches form boundaries between the plates of the crust.

Some different types of folds and faults.

anticline or upfold
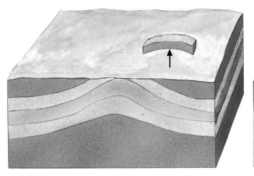

syncline or down fold
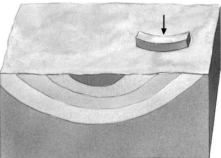

thrust fault: fold has fractured
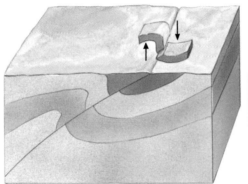

normal fault: rocks have fractured and stretched
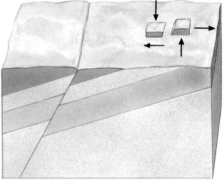

reverse fault: rocks have fractured and been pushed together
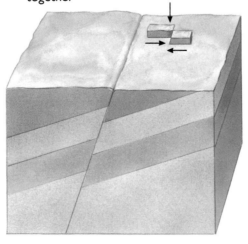

rift valley: ground sinks between two faults
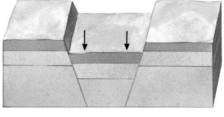

horst: ground pushed up between two faults

Moving Continents

The plates making up the Earth's crust join together to form a mosaic that covers the entire surface of the globe. The plates and the continents that they carry are constantly moving, but so slowly as to pass unnoticed, except by scientists who study the movements.

Spreading and melting

At some plate boundaries, called spreading ridges, convection currents in the Earth's interior cause new crust to rise up from below the surface and to spread out on either side of the central rift. The spreading ridges are mostly beneath the oceans, for example the mid-Atlantic ridge, which divides the Atlantic ocean floor from north to south. At other boundaries, called subduction zones, crust is pushed downwards as two plates move towards each other and one pushes the other beneath it. One example is the west coast of North America, where the Pacific plate is gradually sinking below the plate of the North American continent. At great depths the old crust melts under the heat of the Earth's interior.

Plate boundaries are zones where the crust is likely to be subjected to pressure, stress and shocks. Most earthquakes occur on or close to a plate boundary. Fracturing of the crust along boundaries allows magma or molten rock to reach the surface under pressure, forming volcanoes.

One large continent

Over a century ago scientists first noticed that the edges of some of the continents seem to 'fit' into each other – particularly Africa and South America, which are an almost perfect match. Moreover the rocks and fossils found on the eastern side of South America match up with those on the western side of Africa. The German geologist Alfred

Below: The plates that make up the Earth's crust are constantly moving away from or towards each other. A few million years from now, a map of the world will look quite different from that of today.

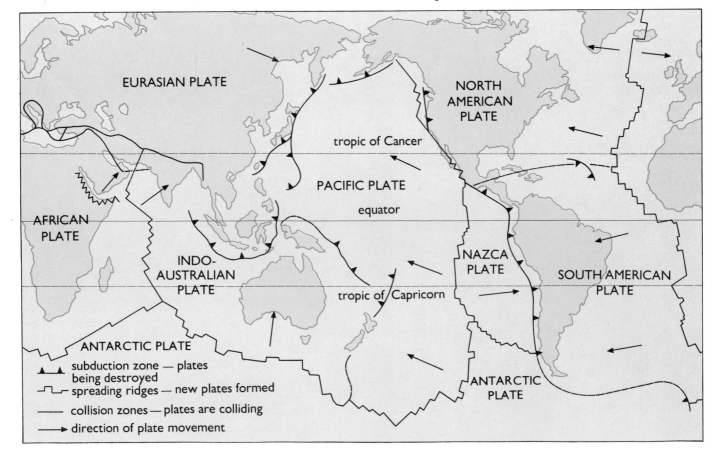

EURASIAN PLATE

NORTH AMERICAN PLATE

tropic of Cancer

PACIFIC PLATE

equator

AFRICAN PLATE

INDO-AUSTRALIAN PLATE

NAZCA PLATE

SOUTH AMERICAN PLATE

tropic of Capricorn

ANTARCTIC PLATE

ANTARCTIC PLATE

subduction zone — plates being destroyed
spreading ridges — new plates formed
collision zones — plates are colliding
direction of plate movement

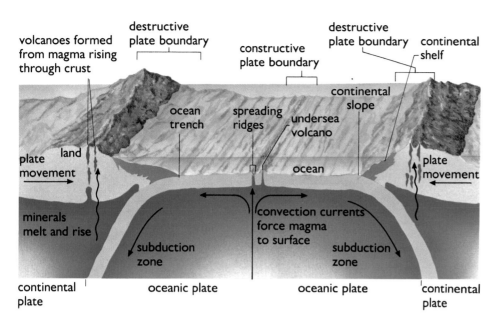

volcanoes formed from magma rising through crust

destructive plate boundary

constructive plate boundary

destructive plate boundary

continental shelf

ocean trench

spreading ridges

undersea volcano

continental slope

plate movement

land

ocean

plate movement

minerals melt and rise

convection currents force magma to surface

subduction zone

subduction zone

continental plate

oceanic plate

oceanic plate

continental plate

Left: The spreading ridges of the ocean floors are zones where new crust is constantly being 'born'. At the ocean margins, deep trenches form where heavy oceanic crust is subducted beneath lighter continental crust and is forced downwards towards the Earth's interior.

Wegener realized that, at one time, Africa and South America had been a single continent, which had since broken into two parts that had drifted away from each other.

Scientists now believe that, until about 200 million years ago, all the continents formed one 'super continent' called Pangaea. This might seem like the very distant past, but is very recent in geological time. Then, Pangaea split into a northern continent, Laurasia, and a southern one, called Gondwanaland. Since that time, plate movements have caused these, in turn, to break up into smaller continents, which have drifted to their present positions on the crust.

The continents have been approximately where they are today for only a few million years, and they continue to drift. Slowly, India is moving northwards and is colliding with the rest of Asia, where it has crumpled the crust to form the folded mountain range of the Himalayas. Australia and Antarctica – at one time both part of Gondwanaland – are moving further apart.

How Pangaea separated into continents.

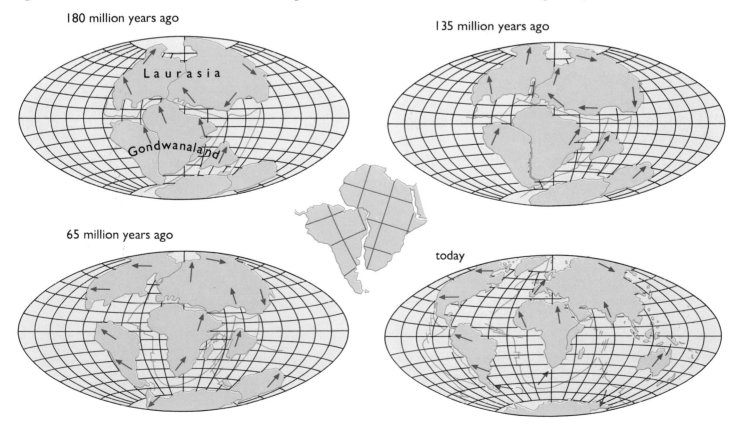

180 million years ago

Laurasia

Gondwanaland

135 million years ago

65 million years ago

today

Rocks and Minerals

'Solid as a rock' is a common saying, but rocks are not always as solid as they seem. The boulders lying at the foot of any cliff show how fragile rocks can sometimes be. Some rocks can easily be broken up into the crystals of which they are formed. Other rocks, formed from layers of sediment, are readily split into thin sheets.

Rocks from crystals

Rocks made up of crystals are called 'igneous' rocks. The crystals are of different shapes, sizes and colours, and a strong blow with a hammer often makes them fall away.

The crystals are the minerals of which the rock is composed.

Igneous rocks (the name is from the Latin for 'fire') are formed from hot molten magma within the Earth's interior. Magma can break through to the surface when a volcano erupts. When the magma cools, its minerals gradually solidify into crystals. Sometimes the magma never reaches the surface, and the minerals cool and solidify slowly in cracks or channels within the crust.

Rocks in layers

Some rocks are made up not of crystals but of fine grains, often seen individually with the help of a magnifying glass, lying in layers or bands. These are sedimentary rocks, formed by the erosion of older rocks by wind, rain, frost, chemicals in the atmosphere, and the heat of the Sun. The eroded rock grains are washed down hillsides and into rivers, which carry them towards the sea. The grains are then laid down as sediments on lake floors, in deltas, or on the sea-bed. Over millions of years, the layers of rock sediment are compressed by other layers laid down on top of them to form solid rock.

The silt and gravels of river beds are examples of sediments that are still too 'young' to have been compressed into solid rock. They are the sedimentary rocks of the future.

Rocks formed under pressure

Another kind of rock – metamorphic rock – has a hard, dense appearance, with no layering or crystals.

sedimentary rocks

volcanic rocks

weathering and erosion

transport by wind and water

deposition

intrusive igneous rocks

magma reservoir

metamorphic rocks

sedimentary rocks

The main types of rock, and how they are formed. Rock material is constantly being recycled within the crust and on the surface to form new rocks.

Metamorphic rocks are formed out of other rocks under great heat and pressure, often during volcanic activity. The intense heat sometimes produces entirely new minerals out of the old ones. The name 'metamorphic' is from the Greek, meaning 'to change form'.

Below: *Quarrying supplies basic materials for the construction industry.*

TYPE OF ROCK	EVERYDAY USE
granite	building materials, gravestones, road chippings
slate	roofing material, paving tiles
limestone	building stone, dry stone walls, cement
chalk	cement
sandstone	building stone, pavements
clay	brick and tile making
coal	fuel
gravel	concrete making

SOME COMMON ROCKS

GRANITE An igneous rock which contains large, distinctive crystals. Granites are formed by the cooling of magma in underground cavities. The principal minerals are quartz (white), feldspar (pink) and mica (black).

LIMESTONE A sedimentary rock with no crystals but containing the remains of shelly sea animals, sometimes entire shells. The rock was formed as animals such as sea snails or corals died and their bones or shells collected in mud on the sea-bed.

SANDSTONE A sedimentary rock formed from layers of sand deposited on beaches or desert basins, or in muddy rivers or deltas.

SLATE A metamorphic rock formed by the compression of shale, a sedimentary rock, under pressure and heat. Its grain runs one way only, and it can be split into very thin sheets.

MARBLE A metamorphic rock formed from the melting and recrystallization of limestone by the Earth's heat.

Volcanoes

A volcano erupts when molten rock bursts with enormous force through a crack or hole in the Earth's crust. Volcanoes are most common at places where weaknesses exist in the crust, especially around the edges of plates, and at 'hot spots' or points in the mantle which are hotter than normal.

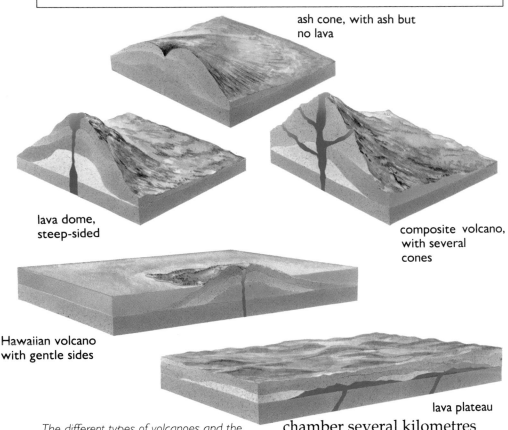

ash cone, with ash but no lava

lava dome, steep-sided

composite volcano, with several cones

Hawaiian volcano with gentle sides

lava plateau

The different types of volcanoes and the materials they throw out.

MOUNT ST HELENS, A VOLCANIC LABORATORY

Scientists can sometimes tell that a volcano is going to erupt by noticing changes in temperature in the area around it. Sometimes the signs are more obvious – the mountainside may begin to bulge, or smoke and steam may be given off. Danger signs like these were noticed on Mount St Helens in the north-western United States in March 1980, and people were warned to leave the area.

Two months later the mountain exploded with such force that one side of it was blown away. The scientists knew that the eruption was coming and spent months filming and studying it and its effects. Mount St Helens became a virtual laboratory for the investigation of volcanoes.

How volcanoes form

Volcanoes result from the build-up of pressure of magma deep within the Earth's crust. When movement of the plates forces part of the crust down into the mantle, the heat causes it to melt. The magma that forms is less dense than the solid rock around it and therefore rises, seeking out lines of weakness in the crust. Together with gases given off, the magma gathers in a chamber several kilometres below the surface. There the pressure builds up steadily until the magma is blasted up through the surface.

An 'active' volcano usually erupts many times after the first explosion. In time, eruptions become less and less frequent, and the volcano is said to be 'dormant'. When all eruptions have stopped, the volcano is called extinct. Sometimes volcanoes thought to be extinct turn out to have been only dormant, and may erupt again.

Different types of volcano

Magma that reaches the surface forms lava, which gradually cools and solidifies. If the lava is thick and sticky, or if it contains many solid pieces of rock and cinders, it forms a steep-sided mountain. Sometimes the magma acts as a plug blocking the channel to the surface. This produces a violent eruption when the plug is blown out.

If the lava is thin and flows easily, it covers a wide area before it becomes solid, building up into a gently sloping 'shield' volcano. Volcanoes of this type are common on the island of Hawaii, USA, and often have large craters. They erupt almost continuously but without real explosions, just throwing out jets of gas and fountains of lava.

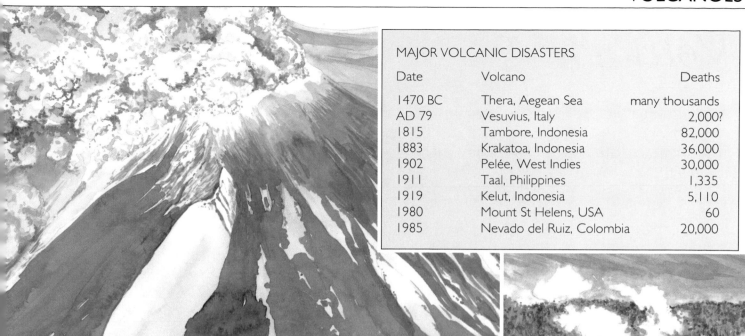

MAJOR VOLCANIC DISASTERS		
Date	Volcano	Deaths
1470 BC	Thera, Aegean Sea	many thousands
AD 79	Vesuvius, Italy	2,000?
1815	Tambore, Indonesia	82,000
1883	Krakatoa, Indonesia	36,000
1902	Pelée, West Indies	30,000
1911	Taal, Philippines	1,335
1919	Kelut, Indonesia	5,110
1980	Mount St Helens, USA	60
1985	Nevado del Ruiz, Colombia	20,000

Dangers and benefits

Volcanoes may cause terrible destruction and loss of life. One of the most violent eruptions of modern times took place on the island of Krakatoa in modern Indonesia in 1883. Dust and clouds reached a height of 28km (18 miles) and the noise from the explosion was heard in northern Australia, over 4,000km (2,500 miles) away. A huge tidal wave or tsunami killed 35,000 people.

Yet volcanoes can have advantages, too. The soil formed from volcanic lava is very fertile and produces plentiful crops. For this reason, millions of people live close to volcanoes despite the risks involved. From studying volcanoes, scientists can learn more about what is happening deep in the Earth.

Right: *Sometimes volcanic activity is limited to fountains of steam and hot water called geysers. In New Zealand geysers are used to provide steam for power stations.*

Below: *Volcanoes erupt from magma chambers just below the surface.*

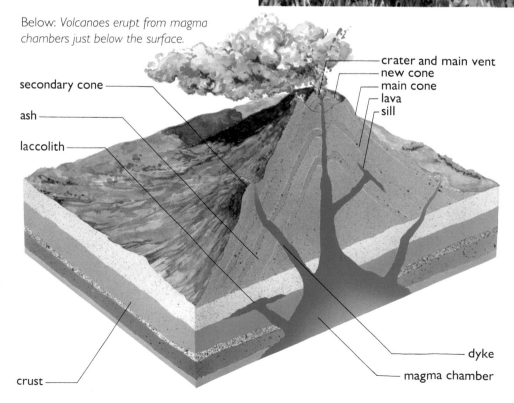

secondary cone

ash

laccolith

crust

crater and main vent
new cone
main cone
lava
sill

dyke

magma chamber

Earthquakes

Earthquakes are caused by stress in the Earth's crust. Pressures from within can produce a build-up of stress in rocks lying against each other. The earthquake 'shock' occurs as the rocks spring back to relieve the stress.

Where earthquakes occur

The regions of the world that are most prone to earthquakes all lie on or near plate boundaries. Many of them are on major fault lines or in areas where volcanoes are likely to occur. Some of the worst earthquakes have been experienced in the countries bordering the Pacific Ocean, such as Japan, and in Central and South America. Greece and other Mediterranean countries, Turkey, Iran, Georgia, Armenia and Azerbaijan also lie on earthquake belts. One of the worst earthquakes in recent

The San Andreas fault and 1906 earthquake.

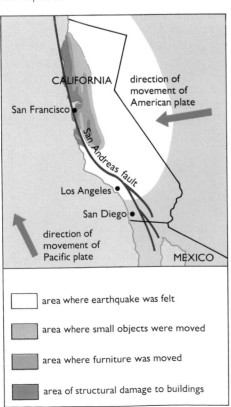

- ☐ area where earthquake was felt
- ☐ area where small objects were moved
- ☐ area where furniture was moved
- ☐ area of structural damage to buildings

THE SAN ANDREAS FAULT

California is one of the world's most earthquake-prone regions. It lies across the San Andreas fault, separating two major world plate boundaries, where the crust is unstable. In 1906 San Francisco suffered one of the worst-ever earthquakes. Seven hundred people were killed, and large parts of the city destroyed. Much of the damage was caused by fires that broke out after the shock.

Since then there have been other earthquakes in California, for example in 1988, but they were not as bad as the San Francisco one. Scientists think that before very long, the area will experience another major earthquake whose effects will be even worse than the 1906 shock. This is because California is now much more populated, so more towns and cities would be at risk. Structures like elevated motorways would be brought crashing down, and the falling glass from tall office buildings would cause death and injury on a huge scale.

In other ways California's cities are better prepared than they were in 1906. Many buildings are more solidly constructed, and there are well-trained emergency and rescue services available to cope with a disaster.

MAJOR EARTHQUAKES		Numbers Killed
1556	Shaanxi, China	830,000
1730	Hokkaido, Japan	137,000
1737	Calcutta, India	300,000
1755	Lisbon, Portugal	60,000
1868	Ecuador and N. Peru	40,000
1906	Valparaiso, Chile	22,000
1906	San Francisco, USA	700
1908	Messina, Italy	77,000
1915	Avezzano, Italy	30,000
1920	Gansu, China	180,000
1923	Yokohama, Japan	143,000
1927	Nan Shan, China	200,000
1931	Napier, New Zealand	250
1932	Gansu, China	70,000
1934	Nepal	11,000
1935	Quetta, Pakistan	30,000
1939	Erzincan, Turkey	30,000
1960	Agadir, Morocco	12,000
1963	Skopje, Yugoslavia	1,000
1964	Anchorage, Alaska	100
1968	N.E. Iran	12,000
1970	N. Peru	67,000
1972	Managua, Nicaragua	7,000
1974	N. Pakistan	10,000
1976	Tangshan, China	650,000
1978	Tabas, Iran	11,000
1980	El Asnam, Algeria	20,000
1985	Mexico	10,000
1988	Armenia	55,000
1990	N. Iran	50,000

years occurred in 1988 in Armenia, in which large parts of the city of Leninakan were destroyed. But even countries very distant from plate boundaries – such as Britain – can experience occasional minor earth tremors.

Measuring and locating earthquakes

The point in the crust where the shock occurs is called the focus of the earthquake. The point immediately above it on the surface is known as the epicentre. Some shock waves travel in a straight line through the crust, while others travel more slowly, close to the surface. The waves can be detected by a seismograph, an instrument in which a pen moves over a sheet of paper attached to a rotating drum. The vibration from the distant earthquake makes the pen vibrate and record the shock.

The intensity of earthquakes is measured by the Richter scale (named after its inventor). On the Richter scale an earthquake that records a value of 6 releases 30 times as much energy as one with a value of 5. But these are only mild shocks. A severe earthquake will measure 8 or even 9 on the Richter scale.

Earthquake damage

Earthquakes can claim many lives and cause an enormous amount of damage to property and infrastructure. Mild earthquakes may do no more than make floors and walls vibrate or make pictures on walls move. Severe earthquakes, however, can cause the collapse of buildings, the destruction of roads and railways, and the loss of water and power supplies. People may die from being trapped under rubble, in fires or explosions, or from the disease and starvation that may follow when the earthquake destroys essential services.

Left: *The damage from an earthquake in a built-up area. Severe earthquakes can reduce parts of cities to rubble.*

Below: *How seismic waves spread after an earthquake.*

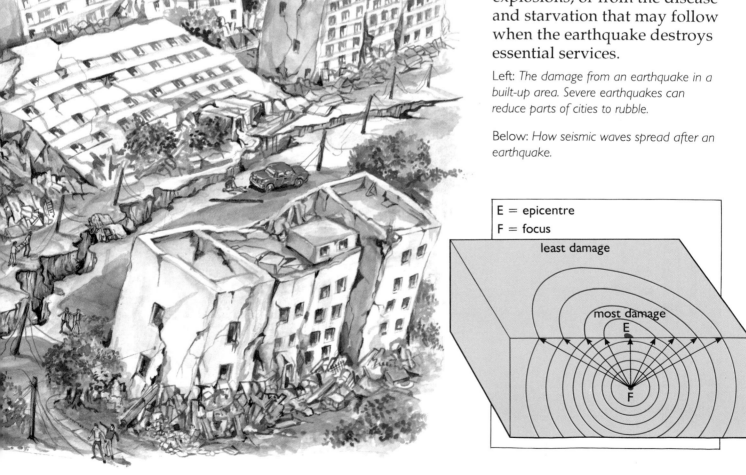

E = epicentre
F = focus
least damage
most damage
E
F

Measuring the Earth

Seen from space, the Earth has no top or bottom or left and right. This makes it very difficult for us to refer to places in relation to each other, as descriptions such as 'above' or 'below' or 'to the right of' become meaningless. To overcome this problem an imaginary grid is spread over the whole of the Earth's surface, and each place is given a numbered reference on the grid.

Latitude and longitude

The grid has parallels of latitude, which measure distance north and south of the equator. Latitude is measured in degrees. The equator is at latitude zero degrees (written 0°) and the poles are at latitudes 90 degrees north or south (written 90° N or S). Each degree is divided into sixty minutes (written 60').

Lines of longitude, or meridians, measure distances east to west. These lines are not parallel but meet at the north and south poles. The lines are numbered in degrees east or west of a zero degree line that runs through the Greenwich Observatory in London. The 180-degree line of longitude is on the opposite side of the Earth from the Greenwich meridian. It is also the International Date Line, dividing areas of the world with different dates from each other.

When used together, lines of latitude and longitude enable any place on the Earth's surface to be accurately located, and to be given a unique reference.

Map projections

To help to understand map-making, the surface of the Earth can be thought of as the skin of an orange. If the orange is peeled and the peel is flattened and spread out, it cannot be made into a whole sheet without creating a lot of gaps; this also applies in the case of the Earth.

Map projections are a way of overcoming this problem. An imaginary source of light from within the globe projects the Earth's surface on to a plane wrapped around the outside of the globe. This makes the globe into a map, but always involves some distortion of shape or area. For example, in a cylindrical projection, in which the Earth is projected on to a cylinder, the whole Earth is seen on one map but lines of longitude are shown as parallels. This makes the polar areas appear to be much wider from east to west than they really are.

Lines of latitude and longitude provide a reference system by which the exact location of any point on the Earth's surface can be pinpointed.

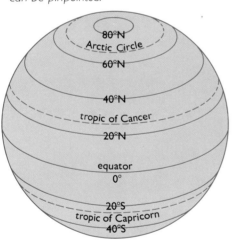

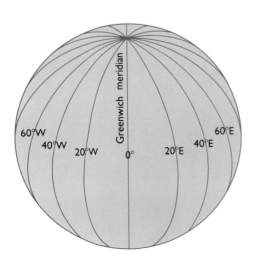

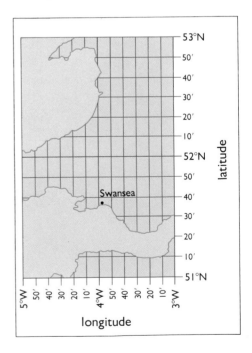

How to give a reference of latitude and longitude. Swansea, Wales, is at 51°38' N, 3°57' W. At this latitude the longitude reading is correct to about 1.16km (0.72 miles); at the equator 1 minute is correct to 1.86km (1.16 miles).

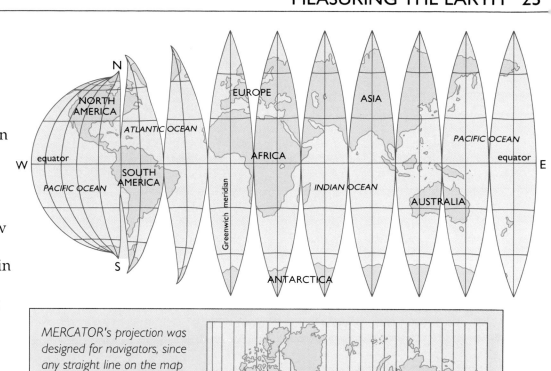

Right: A map of the Earth made by unpeeling strips from the Earth's surface would not be very helpful.

Monitoring the Earth

In the modern world people require up-to-date information about the character of the Earth's surface. Maps and plans need to be revised regularly to keep pace with changes. In built-up areas new buildings and roads are appearing all the time, while in the country agricultural practices can also bring about rapid changes in the landscape.

To keep pace with these developments, modern map-making uses a combination of techniques and information, including photographs from aircraft and detailed ground surveying. Satellites can now scan huge areas of the Earth's surface in great detail. The US Landsat satellites are constantly monitoring the Earth and recording information, sending back updated pictures to ground stations every 16 days. The information received is processed by computers and stored until it is needed.

Such information enables scientists to monitor, for instance, the destruction of tropical rain forests, the changes in the positions of desert margins, and the movement of oil-slicks if a tanker runs aground. Satellite information can also help to discover new mineral resources, and to monitor global warming. The Earth now holds far fewer secrets than it did in the past.

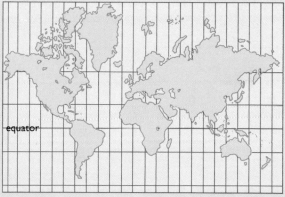

MERCATOR's projection was designed for navigators, since any straight line on the map gives the required compass bearing. However, it makes the continents of the northern hemisphere seem much larger than they really are.

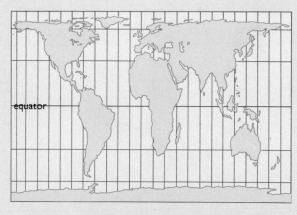

PETERS' projection shows land masses in their correct relative sizes, but makes their shapes look very unfamiliar.

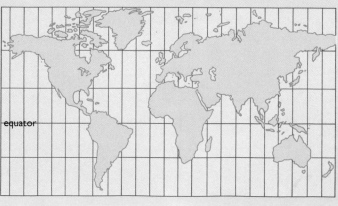

GALL's projection compromises between accuracy of shape and area, and is often used for general world maps in atlases.

References

Continental drift The theory that all the continents were once joined together as a single continent and have since drifted apart.

Core The central zone of the Earth. The inner core, 1,370km (860 miles) thick, is solid; the outer core, about 2,100km (1,300 miles) thick, is liquid. The core consists mostly of iron.

Crust The outer skin of the Earth. Its thickness varies from as little as 6km (less than 4 miles) under the oceans to 40km (25 miles) under the continents. It has continental (granitic), and oceanic (basaltic) layers.

Earthquake A shock or disturbance caused by tension and stress in the crust.

Epicentre The point on the surface directly above the focus (source) of an earthquake.

Equator An imaginary line round the middle of the Earth at equal distance from the poles.

Equinox Time of the year when the Sun is overhead at the equator and day and night are of equal length. Equinoxes occur on 21 March and 21 September.

Faulting Fracturing of the Earth's crust caused by stresses and pressures.

Focus The source of an earthquake; the place in the crust where the shock occurs.

Folding Crumpling of the Earth's crust caused by stresses and pressures. Folding on a continental scale produces 'fold mountains'.

Gaia theory The idea that life on Earth creates the conditions that it needs for its own survival.

Geology The science of the Earth's structure, its crust and its rocks. Geologists study rocks, minerals and fossils (remains of creatures found in rocks), and disturbances to the crust such as earthquakes and volcanoes.

Geyser A volcanic-type eruption which produces only steam and hot water.

Hemisphere One half of the Earth lying to the north (northern hemisphere) or south (southern hemisphere) of the equator.

Ice Ages The Pleistocene geological period, when ice sheets and glaciers covered much of the northern hemisphere.

International Date Line An imaginary line near the 180th meridian used to determine the day or date of different parts of the globe. *See* **Longitude.**

Latitude An imaginary line parallel to the equator used to measure distance. *See* **Longitude.**

Lava Magma that has reached the surface during a volcanic eruption.

Longitude An imaginary line across the Earth's surface joining the north and south poles. Lines of longitude (also called meridians) measure distance from a 'base' meridian running through the Greenwich Observatory in London. *See* **Latitude.**

Magma Molten rock material within the crust. Under pressure, it is forced towards the Earth's surface along faults or weak lines in the crust.

Mantle The zone of the Earth outside the core. It is about 2,900km (1,800 miles) thick.

Map projection A way of representing the Earth's curved surfaces on a flat, plane surface in the form of a map.

Mineral The chemical, metallic, or crystalline substances from which rocks are formed.

Orogeny A period in the Earth's history when ranges of mountains were formed by folding and crumpling of the crust. There were three principal orogenies (Caledonian, Hercynian and Alpine).

Plate A part of the Earth's crust. The movement of crustal plates is related to earthquakes, volcanoes and mountain building.

Plateau A high, relatively level surface formed of old, hard, rocks; sometimes called a tableland.

Radioactive decay The natural decay of radioactive isotopes in rocks. It has helped understanding of the early history of the Earth.

Radiocarbon dating A method of rock dating based on the rate of decay of the isotope carbon-14, which is present in fossilized animal and plant remains.

Richter scale The scale on which earthquake shocks are measured.

Rift valley A valley formed from land slumping between two parallel faults.

Rock The solid part of the Earth's crust beneath the soil. Rocks are described as igneous, sedimentary or metamorphic, depending on how they are formed.

Seismograph An instrument used for detecting earthquake shocks.

Solar system A small part of the Milky Way, one of countless galaxies in the universe.

Solstice The time of the year when the Earth is closest to the Sun (summer solstice) or farthest from it (winter solstice). In the northern hemisphere these occur on 21 June and 21 December.

Spreading ridge A rift along the Earth's crust where new plate material rises up and then spreads out to form new crust. The spreading ridges divide up the main ocean basins.

Subduction zone A trench or zone where the edges of crustal plates are deflected downwards towards the Earth's interior.

Tropic The parallel of latitude 23° 27' north of the equator (tropic of Cancer) or south of the equator (tropic of Capricorn).

Tsunami A giant tidal wave produced by a shock in the ocean floor caused by an earthquake or a volcanic eruption.

Volcano An opening in the Earth's crust through which magma reaches the surface. Volcanoes are classified according to their shape, their structure, and the type of material they eject.

The Shape of the Land

Relief and Rocks

Flat areas occupy only a very small part of the Earth's surface. Most of it is sloping, giving the surface a noticeable shape called relief. Sometimes the slope is very gentle, but often it is very steep, producing hills, mountains, valleys, basins or gorges. In these areas the relief of the land is often very pronounced.

Contour lines

Contours are lines drawn on maps to join surfaces with the same height. They are spaced to represent regular intervals, for example a change in height of 10m (33ft). Careful study of contours allows a picture of the relief of the land to be built up. For instance, contours that form a series of rings with the highest value contours in the middle indicate a hill. Other relief features can also be identified from the shape of the contour lines.

Granite

Hard, resistant rocks such as granite often produce bold, distinctive shapes in the landscape. Granite is formed from magma that has forced its way into great gaps in the Earth's crust and then cooled and solidified deep down before it could reach the surface. Where the softer rocks overlying the granite mass have been worn away they leave it upstanding as a range of hills. The bare rock faces are then attacked by the rain and frost and sometimes worn into strange shapes, like the tor in the illustration. This tor looks like a pile of stones built up one on top of the other, but in fact it is a single block of stone. Tors are common on granite uplands in south-west England, such as Dartmoor and Bodmin Moor.

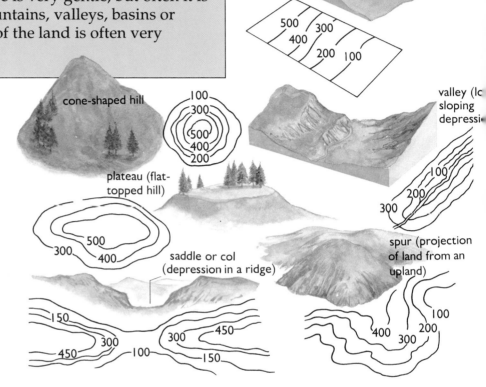

convex slope (slope gentler near the top)

cone-shaped hill

plateau (flat-topped hill)

saddle or col (depression in a ridge)

valley (lo sloping depressi

spur (projection of land from an upland)

Above: *Some relief features with their contour lines.*

Below: *A tor on Dartmoor. Tors are granite boulders weathered into strange shapes.*

Chalk

A layer, or bed, of sedimentary rock is called a stratum (plural strata). Originally strata were laid down horizontally on the floor of the sea or a lake, but have usually been tilted by later Earth movements. Where a stratum reaches the surface it is said to outcrop. An outcrop of chalk often forms an escarpment, that is a ridge with a steep scarp slope and gentle dip slope. The diagram shows typical scarpland scenery, with escarpments of both chalk and limestone separated by low-lying clay vales. Much of the landscape of south-eastern England consists of scarps and vales. The Paris basin of northern France is another scarp and vale landscape.

Chalk is a permeable rock, which means that it holds water. Where the chalk is underlain by a non-permeable rock such as clay, the chalk becomes an aquifer, or water-bearing rock. Water can be pumped up from chalk through wells, but may also reach the surface at springs along the foot of the scarp and dip slopes at the clay boundary.

Limestone

Limestone is another permeable rock. Because water readily seeps down through cracks in the rock (called joints), limestone surfaces are usually dry. Some limestone surfaces form what is known as pavements. These consist of ridges (called clints) that are cut by 'grykes' (deep cracks or fissures). The fissures are

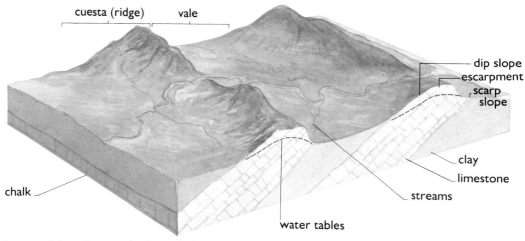

formed by the rock dissolving in water that has penetrated downwards through the joints.

Rivers on limestone sometimes disappear down sink holes into systems of underground caverns and tunnels. Such caverns may contain stalagmites, icicle-like deposits of calcium carbonate that grow upwards from the

Below: Limestone gives rise to pavements, and to underground caverns with stalactites and stalagmites.

Above: Chalk outcrops produce escarpments separated by clay vales.

ground. Stalactites are similar, but hang down from the cavern roof.

The moorlands of North Yorkshire in England have stretches of limestone pavement with underground cave systems. So too, on a larger scale, do the Causses region of the Massif Central in France, and the Karst region of Slovenia.

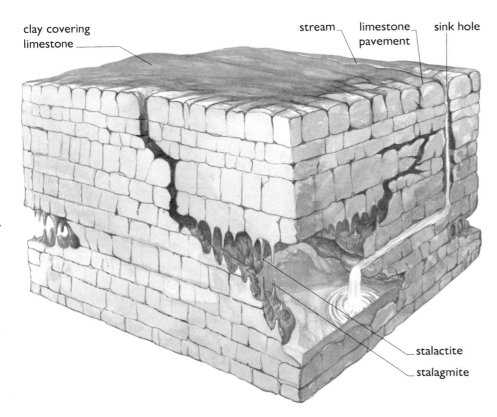

Weathering and Landslides

The writing on gravestones in a churchyard is sometimes very difficult to read. Although the inscriptions were clear enough many years ago, they are very faded now because they have been weathered by the elements. Stone sculptures and carvings that are exposed to the atmosphere are affected in the same way.

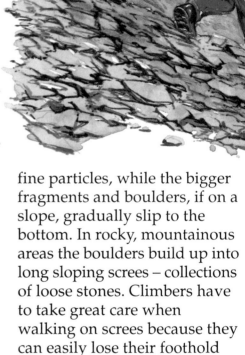

Left: *This statue has been badly weathered. It is difficult to make out its original detail.*

Weathering

Rock surfaces also suffer from weathering. Rocks are attacked by the atmosphere, sun and rain. In cold weather frost and ice get into the pore spaces and into cracks and crevices. The water expands as it freezes, and pieces of rock, sometimes the size of boulders, can break off. In deserts, the hot sun beating down on the bare rocks causes the different minerals of which the rock is formed to expand at different rates, making the surface break up and crumble.

Chemicals in the atmosphere also attack rocks. Acids in the air convert the iron in rocks into a surface layer of rust, which crumbles. Other acids, from the roots of plants, attack the surface of the rock crevice in which the plant may be growing, by changing the rock minerals into salts, which are dissolved and washed out by rainwater.

Weathering produces a debris of rock fragments and finer silt-like material. Rainwater washes away the fine particles, while the bigger fragments and boulders, if on a slope, gradually slip to the bottom. In rocky, mountainous areas the boulders build up into long sloping screes – collections of loose stones. Climbers have to take great care when walking on screes because they can easily lose their foothold and accidentally fall.

Landslides

A landslide is a fast movement of large masses of rock and soil down a slope. Landslides happen when hill slopes become unstable. The build-up before the landslide may take many years, perhaps even centuries, as more and more loose material accumulates on the slope. Heavy rainfall can also saturate the underlying

Climbing on screes can be dangerous. Even experienced climbers have to be careful.

MUDFLOW AT ARMERO

Mudflows can be as devastating as landslides. In 1985 a disastrous mudflow occurred at Armero, a small town in Colombia in the Andean mountain range, close to the volcano of Nevado del Ruiz. When the volcano erupted the heat melted the ice-cap on the mountain. The huge surge of melting water picked up masses of ash and rock boulders, turning it into a vast tongue of slurry. Helped by heavy rainfall, this mudflow rushed down the valley, reaching a speed of 90km/h (56mph). It buried Armero in a mass of mud up to 5m (16ft) thick, killing some 23,000 people.

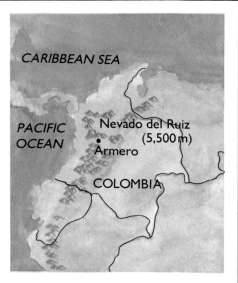

Below: *How the mudflow from Nevado del Ruiz destroyed the town of Armero.*

ground, allowing the top surface to slide downhill as a mudflow.

The landslide itself is usually triggered by sudden vibration, perhaps caused by an earth tremor some distance away. Human activities such as setting off explosions in quarries, or even vibration from heavy vehicles, can also start a landslide if the slope is already unstable.

People living in mountain areas – especially in places of crustal instability that are prone to earth tremors – are under constant threat from landslides. Sometimes these cause only the loss of small fields or pastures, but some landslides can destroy entire villages, and many lives may be lost.

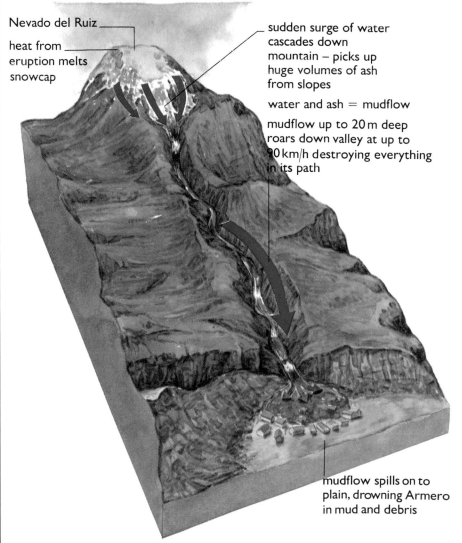

Nevado del Ruiz

heat from eruption melts snowcap

sudden surge of water cascades down mountain – picks up huge volumes of ash from slopes

water and ash = mudflow

mudflow up to 20 m deep roars down valley at up to 90 km/h destroying everything in its path

mudflow spills on to plain, drowning Armero in mud and debris

The Work of Rivers

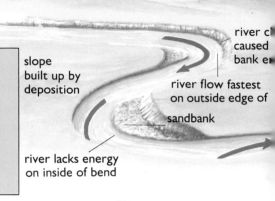

Most of the Earth's surface is drained by rivers. Even deserts have river valleys, although they may seldom contain water. Millions of people depend on rivers for their livelihoods, while many others depend on them less directly, in other ways. Today most of the world's major river basins are controlled to meet human needs.

river c
caused
bank e

slope
built up by
deposition

river flow fastest
on outside edge of

sandbank

river lacks energy
on inside of bend

THE LONGEST RIVERS	kilometres	miles
Nile, Africa	6,690	4,157
Amazon, S. America	6,280	3,903
Mississippi–Missouri, N. America	6,270	3,896
Yangtze, Asia	4,990	3,101
Zaire, Africa	4,670	2,902
Amur, Asia	4,410	2,740
Hwang-ho (Yellow), Asia	4,350	2,704
Lena, Asia	4,260	2,647
Mekong, Asia	4,180	2,598
Niger, Africa	4,180	2,598

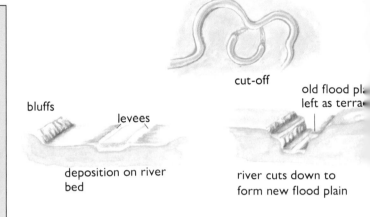

cut-off

old flood pl
left as terra

bluffs

levees

deposition on river
bed

river cuts down to
form new flood plain

A river basin

Rivers form branching networks. The area drained by a river network is called its drainage basin or catchment area. The area boundary is known as the watershed. Within the drainage basin smaller streams, called tributaries, unite with the larger streams, and these eventually join together to form one main stream or river.

Rivers usually have their sources in hilly or mountainous regions, emerging from springs or seeping out of the soil high on the slopes. Glacial streams appear as meltwater from permanent snow and the snouts of glaciers. Steep gradients give the river energy, which it uses in tumbling over

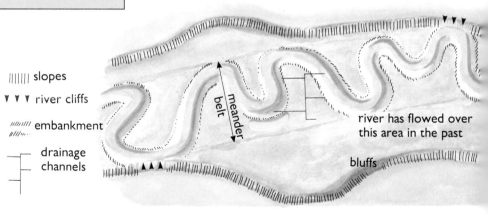

slopes
river cliffs
embankment
drainage channels

meander belt

river has flowed over
this area in the past

bluffs

Some of the features of a river valley.

rocky boulders, waterfalls and rapids. In heavy storms the river level rises, and the water has enough power to carry stones and boulders along its bed, and to erode its banks and any other obstacles it finds. The material transported by the river is called its load.

In its lower course the river has a very gentle gradient. It

often follows a winding, wandering course, creating meanders. It may not be able to carry all its load of sediment, and much of it, especially the coarser material such as boulders and pebbles, is dumped on the river bed. Periodically, especially after prolonged heavy rainfall, the river may burst its banks, spreading flood waters and silt over a wide area, called the flood plain.

The river's end

At its estuary the river finds its outlet to the sea. There water from the river mixes with the denser, saline (salty) sea water. Heavy tides may raise water levels in the estuary, sometimes causing flooding if high tides coincide with storm conditions. Many rivers reach the sea as deltas. Within the delta, the river breaks up into a large number of tiny channels, which wind to and fro over enormous expanses of silt carried down by the river from many kilometres inland. Eventually, islands may form from this deposition as land extends slowly into the sea.

In millions of years' time, the silt deposited from rivers on the sea-bed may be uplifted to form new mountain ranges.

The world's main river basins.

Bennet WAC
Bratsk
Zeya
Krasnoyarsk
Sayano
Shushenskaya
Mackenzie
Columbia
Mississippi
Colorado
Mica
Grand Coulee
Hoover
Imperial
Parker
Orinoco
Amazon
Parana
Aswan
Akosombo
Guri
Chivor
Niger
Volta
Congo
Zambezi
Orange
Verwoerd
Nile
Tigris-Euphrates
Indus
Ganges
Volga
Ob
Yenisey
Lena
Amur
Hwang-ho
Yangtze
Carbora Bassa
Kariba
Murray-Darling
Burrinjuck
Wyangara

● dams and reservoirs

THE NILE: A MIGHTY RIVER

Besides being the world's longest river, the Nile is also an international river, flowing through several countries. It rises in the mountains of Ethiopia and Uganda as the Blue Nile and White Nile, and then flows northwards through the Sudan as the Nile. The last country to be reached, Egypt, is entirely dependent on the Nile since almost the whole of its population lives along its banks.

Every year, for thousands of years, the river flooded naturally, spreading water and fertile silt on the nearby fields. Farmers built earthen banks around their small fields to catch the flood waters, releasing the water gradually to irrigate their crops.

Today the Nile is much more controlled. With the help of modern technology and foreign aid, Egypt built the Aswan High Dam, opened in 1971. The huge reservoir of Lake Nasser, 500km (310 miles) long,

The mighty Aswan High Dam.

allows water to be used for irrigation continuously. The Aswan Dam has increased food output, making irrigation possible all the year round, and allowing the reclamation of 400,000ha (1,500 square miles) of desert.

However, the Aswan Dam has greatly reduced the river's flow downstream, so that very little fresh water reaches the Mediterranean sea. Salt water spreading inland is now killing crops. In the Sudan the Jonglei Canal is being built to bypass a large area of marshland to reduce the amount of water lost by the Nile from evaporation and to increase its flow once more.

Ice and Glaciation

More than a million years ago large areas of the northern continents were covered by ice sheets and glaciers. Since then the ice has several times melted and retreated, and then returned. Today vast ice sheets still cover Antarctica and Greenland, while glaciers form in mountainous and very cold areas such as Alaska, Scandinavia, the Alps and the Himalayas. If this ice were to melt, many cities and populations would be drowned by the rising sea-level.

How ice caps form and spread.

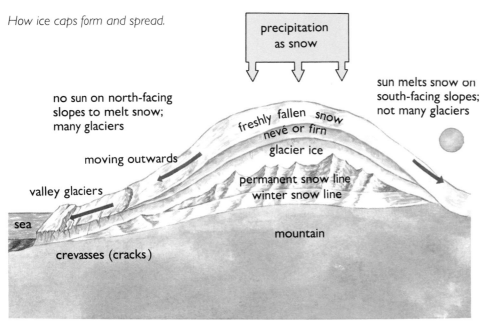

precipitation as snow

no sun on north-facing slopes to melt snow; many glaciers

sun melts snow on south-facing slopes; not many glaciers

freshly fallen snow

nevé or firn

moving outwards

glacier ice

valley glaciers

permanent snow line

winter snow line

sea

mountain

crevasses (cracks)

How glaciers form

Glaciers begin high on mountainsides where it is too cold for fallen snow to melt. The snow that gathers in hollows becomes thicker and thicker and is gradually compressed into layers of ice. The growing ice mass eventually spills out of the hollow, gouging it out into a deep 'corrie' as it does so. Ice from several corries joins together to form a glacier, which moves slowly down the mountainside, often following an old river valley which it deepens into a U-shape.

Weathered rock fragments from the slopes above tumble into the glacier and are carried along. This debris is known as moraine.

How glaciers end

Some glaciers spread out into thin ice sheets when they reach the lower ground at the foot of the mountain. Others melt before they arrive there, dumping great heaps of stones and boulders they have been carrying. Long ridges of sand, gravel and boulders called terminal moraines sometimes mark the furthest point that

was reached by the ice before it began to melt. Streams form on top of and inside the ice, carrying pebbles and silt which are deposited in sheets or fans beyond the edge of the melting ice.

Big boulders, known as erratics, can sometimes be found scattered across glaciated areas. The rock type of the erratic can be matched up with rock outcrops many kilometres away, showing that the boulder must have been carried by the ice over a great distance.

Sometimes glaciers will not have melted even by the time they reach the coast. When this happens, great masses of ice break off and drift away into the sea to become icebergs.

Fiords

Fiords are long, deep, coastal inlets, which often extend far inland. They were once glaciated valleys, gouged by

A glacial erratic carried many kilometres from its source area.

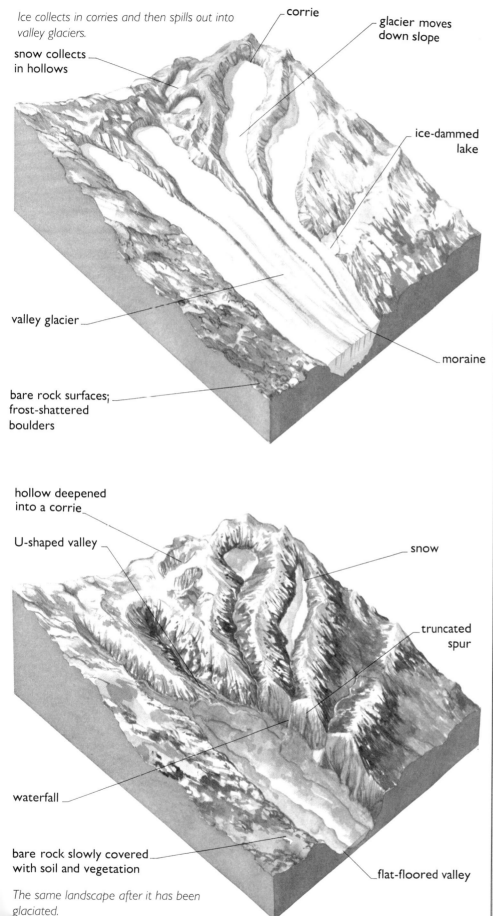

Ice collects in corries and then spills out into valley glaciers.

snow collects in hollows

corrie

glacier moves down slope

ice-dammed lake

valley glacier

moraine

bare rock surfaces; frost-shattered boulders

hollow deepened into a corrie

U-shaped valley

snow

truncated spur

waterfall

bare rock slowly covered with soil and vegetation

flat-floored valley

The same landscape after it has been glaciated.

the moving ice to depths of more than 100m (330ft). When the ice melted, the valleys were drowned by the sea. Some of the longest fiords are in Norway, but fiord coasts also occur in Alaska and New Zealand. The sea lochs of western Scotland are fiords.

THE GREENLAND ICEBERGS

Greenland produces many icebergs every year. As the glaciers reach the coast, the icebergs break off and drift away on the sea currents. One glacier alone, the Jakobshaven Isfiord on the west coast, carries 11 per cent of Greenland's total ice discharge into the sea. It produces some 30 new icebergs every year.

Sea currents carry the Greenland icebergs southwards towards the coast of Labrador. Here they may be a hazard to transatlantic shipping. A regular patrol in the region warns ships of iceberg movements.

In April 1912 a new ocean liner, the *Titanic*, was making its maiden voyage across the Atlantic. Its designers claimed it was unsinkable. But one night the *Titanic* hit an iceberg, and sank shortly afterwards with the loss of 1,500 lives. The wreck was not found until 1985.

An iceberg off the coast of Greenland.

Coasts

Everywhere coastlines are constantly changing. Some coastlines retreat because of erosion, that is wearing away by the sea; others advance seawards because they are being built up by deposits of sand and pebbles. A stretch of coast can change noticeably even within a human lifetime.

Coastal erosion

Coasts are eroded by wave attack. During a heavy storm the waves are driven on by the strong winds that have been blowing over them for long distances. As the waves break on to a rocky shore, they hurl huge masses of water and pebbles against the cliff face. The pressure of sea-water forced into cracks and crevices causes the rock to splinter and break away. Also, heavy rain can attack cliffs of soft rocks, which become sodden and crumble away on to the beach.

Waves shape the coastline. Soft rocks are worn back more quickly than harder ones, so that the harder rocks stand out into the sea as headlands. If the headlands are attacked by the sea from both sides, cracks may be enlarged into caves, which in time will be worn all the way through the headlands to form arches. Eventually the roof of the arch may collapse, leaving a stump, or stack.

How coastlines are built up

Gentler waves, together with currents and tides, carry sand and sediment along the coast and then dump them on the shore. This helps to build up the coastline, creating beaches and sand dunes. Sometimes the transport of sediment along the coast is interrupted by the mouth of a river. Then, the sediment is deposited as a long ridge, called a 'spit', lying parallel to the coastline and deflecting the river's outlet for several miles.

Ups and downs

Movements of the Earth also contribute to shaping coasts. The surface of north-western Scotland, once covered by masses of ice during the Ice Age, is gradually rising because the melting of the ice-caps has released the pressure

How the sea can shape headlands, producing arches and stacks.

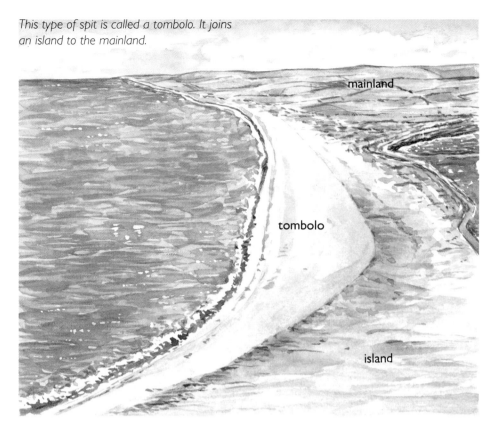

This type of spit is called a tombolo. It joins an island to the mainland.

mainland

tombolo

island

on the ground. Parts of its coastline are advancing seawards, in some cases by several millimetres each year.

By contrast, in southern England the rise in sea-level, brought about by the melting of the ice-caps, has submerged much of the coast, causing it to retreat. Submergence around upland areas like Devon has produced many rias, or drowned river valleys.

Some major cities of the world are on sinking coastlines. London, for example, is sinking at the rate of 2mm (0.08in) a year. If climatic warming over the next few decades brings about a further rise in sea-level, much of London will be submerged.

THE THAMES FLOOD BARRIER

Besides being on sinking land, London also faces the problem of tidal surges from the North Sea. These could cause a build-up of water in the Thames estuary, flooding much of the capital. In 1953 disaster was narrowly avoided when flood waters that killed 300 people on the east coast of England and the Thames estuary stopped short of London. A similar disaster today might put 1.5 million people at risk.

London's answer has been to build a flood barrier across the Thames, stretching 520 metres (1,705 feet) bank to bank. Under normal conditions the barrier's massive gates (the four main ones each weigh over 3,000 tonnes) rest unseen in curved recesses in the river-bed, allowing shipping to pass through. But if a tidal surge threatens, the gates swing up through 90 degrees to form a steel wall ready to prevent flood waters moving up the river.

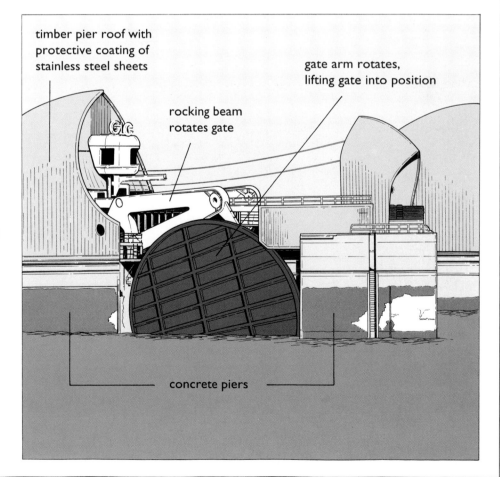

timber pier roof with protective coating of stainless steel sheets

gate arm rotates, lifting gate into position

rocking beam rotates gate

concrete piers

Deserts

Deserts are the Earth's driest places. An area is usually called a desert if it receives less than 250mm (10in) of rain a year, but many deserts receive much less than this. Such conditions are found on over 15 per cent of the Earth's land surface. A further 15 per cent has semi-desert conditions, where there is some vegetation, but it is still too dry for crops to grow.

World deserts

All continents contain deserts. The Sahara is the world's largest desert, stretching across the whole of North Africa. The same desert belt continues across the Red Sea into Saudi Arabia, Iran, Pakistan and north-west India.These are all hot deserts, but there are also cold deserts such as the Gobi in central Asia.

Deserts of sand

To many people, the idea of a hot desert suggests a sea of sand stretching as far as the horizon. Desert sand is built up by the wind into enormous dunes, between which occasional camel trains or convoys of vehicles pick their way along trackways that are soon lost again to the shifting sands.

There are several kinds of sand dune. 'Barchan' dunes make striking shapes. Seen from the air, they form a carpet of crescent-shaped hills with the points of the crescents facing in the direction of the wind. The wind blows sand up the back slope of the barchan and down its sheltered slope, so that the whole dune moves forward. 'Sief' dunes form long ridges parallel to the direction of the wind, which blows along the troughs between the ridges. Like barchans, sief dunes constantly change their position.

Deserts of mountains and rocks

Many deserts, however, are not seas of sand. Some are mountain ranges and plateau

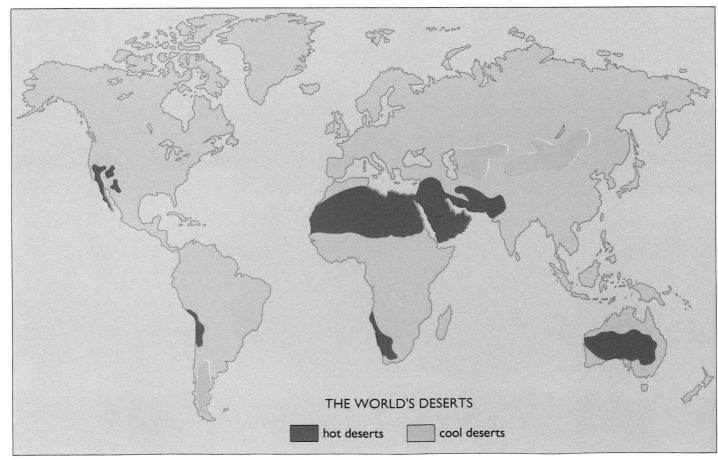

THE WORLD'S DESERTS

hot deserts   cool deserts

surfaces, with craggy rock faces and expanses of broken rock and pebbles. During the day sun makes the rock intensely hot, so that it expands, while at night the temperature falls very steeply and the rock contracts. The expansion and contraction causes rock fragments to splinter off and tumble down the rock faces. There, against the rock faces, the fragments build up into huge cones. As the mountain slopes themselves are steep and angular, it is easy to distinguish the different rock beds in the slope.

Often the mountains have flat plateau tops of hard, resistant rock, which protect the rocks beneath from further wearing away. These plateau surfaces are cut by deep, steeply sloping valleys called wadis or canyons. The wadis are normally dry, but on the rare occasions when it rains, they are converted into raging torrents.

Oases and salt lakes

An oasis is a place in a desert that is made fertile because of the presence of water. Usually oases occur where the water-table reaches the surface. The aquifer (water-retaining rock bed), is kept charged by rain seeping into it from hundreds of kilometres away. Further water can be extracted by sinking wells in the aquifer.

All deserts contain river channels which are occupied by water when it rains. Sometimes there is enough water for several channels to come together and form a lake. Such lakes, known as playas, soon dry out in the heat, but as the water evaporates it leaves behind the salts that it contains. The Great Salt Lake of Utah, USA, has very little water, and consists largely of layers of dried salts.

Above: *An oasis in the Sahara desert, among crescent-shaped sand dunes.*

Below: *The desert in Monument Valley, Utah, USA. These pinnacles, or buttes, are all that is left of the great rock structures that once covered the area. One day these too will have been worn away.*

The Ocean Basins

More than 70 per cent of the Earth's surface is covered with oceans and seas. Stimulated by the Sun's heat, the oceans are constantly circulating around and between the land masses that make up the other 30 per cent. Beneath the oceans the relief of the ocean floor is as varied as that of the continents.

Oceanic mountains and basins

Close to the coasts of the continents are shallow seas going down to depths of 200m (650ft) on the continental shelves. These shelves are really an underwater extension of the continental land masses, and are fed by the masses of sediment washed down on to them by the world's great rivers. They end in steep edges which plunge several hundreds or thousands of metres down to the ocean floors.

The ocean floors form vast underwater plains, broken down the middle by ranges of underwater mountains laid out in a series of great ridges and trenches. It is along these trenches that new crustal material slowly emerges on to the Earth's surface. The ocean floors are also interrupted by ranges of volcanic peaks, which sometimes break the surface as arcs of islands. Near some continental margins the ocean floor plunges yet again,

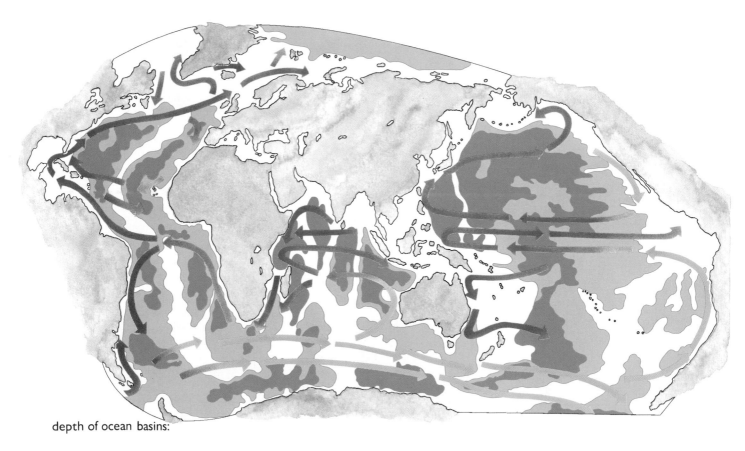

depth of ocean basins:

☐	0–4,000 m
▨	4,000–5,000 m
▧	5,000–7,000 m

➡ warm currents
➡ cold currents

The ocean basins extend to greater depths than many of the world's highest mountains. Ocean currents, which circulate water between basins, are influenced by the Earth's rotation. They help to even out variations in global temperature.

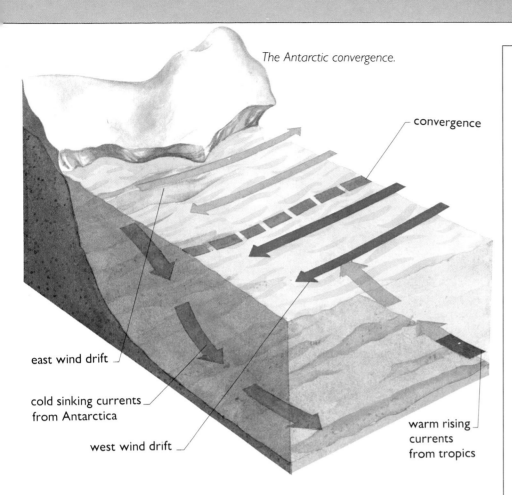

The Antarctic convergence.

convergence

east wind drift

cold sinking currents from Antarctica

west wind drift

warm rising currents from tropics

THE GULF STREAM

The Gulf Stream is one of the principal ocean currents, and is vital to the climate of northern Europe. It begins as a result of solar warming in the region of the Gulf of Mexico. Here the heating of the oceans by hot tropical sun causes the expanding waters to begin to drift towards the poles.

The drifts are deflected by the Earth's west-to-east rotation, and are directed northwards up the eastern side of North America. Some 55 million cubic metres (1,950 million cubic feet) of warm water is moved every second, about 50 times more water than is contained in all the world's rivers.

As the Gulf Stream moves up through the north Atlantic, it warms the winds that blow across it. These winds carry mild air to the countries of north-western Europe, giving them mild winters. That is why places in northern Britain or Norway have much warmer winters than places in eastern Europe at the same latitude.

down to great troughs as much as 11,000m (36,000ft) below sea-level.

Oceanic currents

Along the equator and the tropics the Sun is constantly warming the oceans, setting up huge convection currents on a global scale. The drifting of these warm currents is guided partly by the Earth's rotation, a result of the Coriolis force. Many currents drift towards the poles, moving masses of warm water into colder regions. A counter flow of cold currents moves cooler water from polar to equatorial regions.

In this way the ocean currents act as a vast heat-exchanging system, continuously interchanging warm equatorial and cold polar waters. This exchange is necessary for keeping the Earth at a constant temperature. Without it the equatorial areas would be getting hotter all the time, and polar regions would be getting colder.

ANTARCTIC CURRENTS

Ocean currents support much life on Earth. Around the Antarctic, warm currents from the tropics meet cold Antarctic currents. This is called the Antarctic convergence. The turbulence between the two brings nutrient-rich waters to the surface. Great swarms of krill, a shrimp-like creature, rise to the top and provide the staple food for penguins, seals, squid and whales. Without the convergence the Antarctic chain of life would be impossible.

OCEAN AND SEA AREAS IN 1000 km²	
Pacific Ocean	165,721
Atlantic Ocean	81,660
Indian Ocean	73,442
Arctic Ocean	14,351
Mediterranean Sea	2,966
Bering Sea	2,274
Caribbean Sea	1,942
Mexico, Gulf of	1,813
Okhotsk, Sea of	1,528
East China Sea	1,248
Hudson Bay	1,230
Japan, Sea of	1,049
North Sea	575
Black Sea	448
Red Sea	440
Baltic Sea	422
Persian Sea	238
St Lawrence, Gulf of	236
English Channel and Irish Sea	179
California, Gulf of	161

References

Aquifer A stratum that is permeable, that is, it holds water.

Barchan A crescent-shaped sand dune.

Butte A stump or pinnacle of rock standing high above the surface of a desert.

Catchment area (drainage basin) An area drained by a river and its tributaries.

Cavern An underground chamber in limestone, forming part of a series of passages and tunnels used by underground streams.

Continental shelf The area of shallow seas around the edges of a continent.

Contour A line on a map joining points with the same altitude.

Coriolis force or effect The deflection of the movements of the oceans or air currents caused by the Earth's rotation, which is faster at the equator than at the poles.

Corrie A hollow on a mountainside where snow gathers and forms glacier ice. Corries have steep backwalls. The floor of the corrie is sometimes occupied by a small lake, or tarn.

Delta A triangular-shaped fan of silt at a river's mouth. The river breaks up into a large number of smaller channels, giving the appearance of a bird's foot.

Desert An area where very little, or nothing, can grow; usually somewhere with less than 250mm (10in) of rainfall per year. Many desert areas receive much less than this, having no rain at all for many years.

Erosion The wearing away of the landscape by running water, ice, the wind or the sea.

Erratic A large rock boulder transported by a glacier and dumped at some distance from its origin.

Escarpment A ridge of high ground, usually with a gentle back or dip slope and a steeper scarp slope.

Estuary The mouth of a river; its outlet to the sea.

Fiord A long, deep coastal inlet once occupied by a glacier; a drowned glacial valley.

Headland A portion of coastline protruding outwards into the sea.

Ice Age The Ice Age (or Ice Ages) were the Pleistocene geological period, when ice-caps and glaciers covered much of the northern hemisphere. There were four periods of ice advance, separated by warmer periods called 'interglacials'.

Iceberg A huge floating mass of ice. About eight-ninths of the ice mass is submerged.

Joint A crack in the rock structure. Joints are easily attacked by rain, frost and the sea, which may enlarge them into large fissures. The entire rock surface may then crumble away. *See* **Weathering.**

Landslide A rapid movement of masses of rock and soil down a slope. Landslides are most common in mountain areas. They can be set off by excessive rainfall or an earthquake or any other vibration.

Meander A large loop in the river's course. Sometimes the curve is so severe that the two sides of the meander meet, and the river cuts a channel across the neck. The remains of the old meander are called an oxbow.

Moraine The rock debris carried along by a glacier. Some of it is carried at the edge of the glacier (lateral moraine); other material is in the middle (medial moraine). Medial moraines are formed by two converging glaciers. A terminal moraine is a ridge which marks where the ice front began to melt.

Mudflow A type of landslide where water from rain or rivers mixes with soil and rock fragments to form mud.

Oasis A fertile place in a desert. Oases occur where the water table reaches the surface, so that water can be obtained from an aquifer.

Outcrop The place or area where a rock stratum reaches the surface.

Pavement A bare surface made of limestone. The pavement is broken by long parallel cracks (grykes) separated by ridges (clints).

Relief The shape of the land; the pattern of mountains, hills and valleys; the difference between the high areas and low areas.

Ria A river valley drowned by rising sea-level. Rias form broad, deep estuaries.

Salt lake A lake in a desert consisting of saline water and expanses of salt deposits. The salts are deposited as the water evaporates.

Scree A long straight slope consisting of boulders and stones. The fragments are caused by the wearing away of rock faces at the top of the slope, especially by sun or frost.

Spit A long ridge of sand or shingle projecting into the sea, or out into the mouth of a river.

Stack A stump of rock protruding above the level of the sea; it is often the only remains of an old part of the coastline, the rest having been worn away.

Stalactites and **stalagmites** Long, thin columns of calcium carbonate which hang down from the roof (stalactites) or grow upwards from the ground (stalagmites) in limestone caverns. *See* **Cavern.**

Stratum (pl. strata) A layer or bed of rock. Strata are often formed from sediment laid down in shallow seas or lakes.

Tor A hilltop of craggy rock surface, especially of granite, sometimes weathered into strange shapes.

Watershed The boundary of a catchment area or drainage basin. *See* **Catchment area.**

Weathering The wearing away of rock surfaces by the atmosphere, sun, frost and rain. Some weathering is carried out by the acids present in the atmosphere and in rainwater.

Weather and Climate

Weather Forecasting

How can the weather forecasters tell what the weather will be like? Many people have a story to tell about how the forecast weather turned out to be wrong – sometimes with tragic consequences. Yet the weather people themselves claim that over the years their forecasts have been getting more accurate. Today they can monitor the weather from space as well as from instruments on the ground, using computers to help them piece together all the information.

Weather from space and on the ground

High above the Earth is a weather satellite called 'Meteosat', which always remains over the same spot on the Earth's surface. Meteosat sends back pictures to ground receiving stations every few minutes. Some of these pictures show swirling cloud patterns, from which the meteorologists (weather forecasters) can work out which way the winds are blowing. This helps them to predict which areas will be the next to be affected by cloud and rain. The satellite also sends back infra-red pictures. These show variations in temperature by making warm surfaces appear dark and cold surfaces appear light.

Meteosat cannot 'see' round the curve of the globe to the other side, but other satellites send back pictures of these 'hidden' parts of the world. In this way the meteorologists can build up a complete picture of the world's weather.

Weather forecasts also need the very detailed recordings of weather conditions made by weather stations at ground level. Here a variety of instruments measure temperature, rainfall, humidity, pressure, sunshine, wind speed and wind direction, cloud cover and other weather properties. Accurate readings are taken regularly, and the information is combined to produce a total weather 'picture'. Many weather stations are on ships at sea. Fully automated ground weather stations are also now very common.

The Earth seen from a weather satellite. The white patches are areas of cloud.

Global and regional weather centres

World Weather Watch is a global system which coordinates the many observations and recordings made every day. Four times a day, measurements are taken at 3,000 ground stations and on 4,000 weather ships, which together cover the globe. These measurements and others from aircraft and satellites are passed to Global Meteorological Centres in Washington, Moscow and Melbourne. They, in turn, supply information to regional forecasting centres such as the Meteorological Office in Bracknell, UK.

The forecasters at centres like Bracknell feed the information they receive into computers for analysis. The computers produce large maps, called synoptic charts, which summarize all the known weather information. Using this information, the computers then produce models of how the weather will change further in the near future. Bracknell makes over

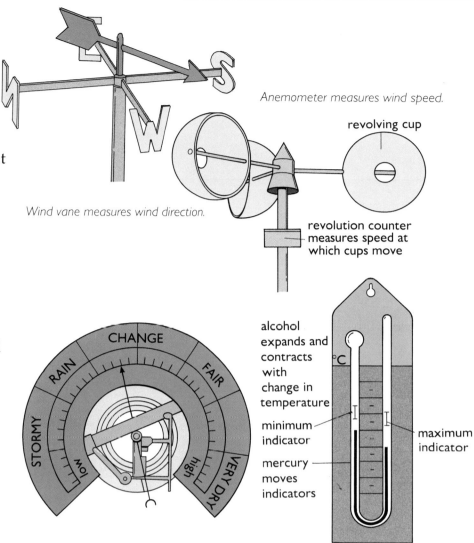

Anemometer measures wind speed.

revolving cup

revolution counter measures speed at which cups move

Wind vane measures wind direction.

Barometer measures atmospheric pressure.

alcohol expands and contracts with change in temperature

minimum indicator

mercury moves indicators

maximum indicator

Maximum and minimum thermometer records the highest and lowest temperatures over a time period.

700 different analyses and forecasts every day, showing, for instance, which way a band of cloud might be expected to move, or which areas are likely to become cold enough to receive snow. The forecasts are then made available to radio and television networks and to the press. Within a few hours of the original information being recorded, the forecast is in the hands of the television presenter.

Right: *Symbols used on some television weather maps.*

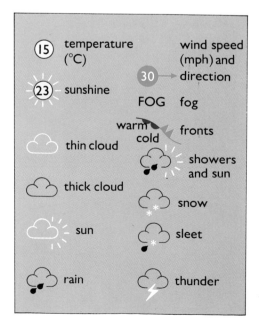

(15) temperature (°C)

wind speed (mph) and direction

30

(23) sunshine

FOG fog

thin cloud

warm cold fronts

thick cloud

showers and sun

sun

snow

sleet

rain

thunder

Sunshine and Showers

'Sunshine and showers' is a phrase commonly used by weather forecasters. Usually it means that we can expect a sunny day, apart from short periods of cloud and rain. The occurrence of showers, or even thunderstorms, depends on convection – hot air rising – during the day.

Sunshine

Warm, sunny weather does not depend just on the Sun shining, but also on how it gives out its heat. During the summer the Sun is out many hours each day, for much of the day at a high angle in the sky. When the Sun's rays fall from a steep angle, their heat output is concentrated on a small area, making the ground hot quickly.

In winter the Sun is only out for a few hours each day. During this brief period it heats the ground from a much lower angle, so that the heat is spread over a wide area. Its heating power is much less, and sometimes hardly enough to melt the overnight frost.

Showers

On warm, sunny days, surfaces like tarmac or concrete can become very hot indeed, and often show a 'heat haze' caused by the hot air rising. The air rises because the heat from the Sun and from the hot surface beneath makes it expand. As it expands it becomes light and buoyant, and rises as invisible bubbles. This process is called convection.

The rising air may contain water vapour (evaporated water) from lakes, streams, the surfaces of plants, or the soil. As the air rises, this water vapour cools and condenses to form clouds. If the air rises further, droplets of water will form. By this time, the sky, which was clear only half an hour ago, will be overcast, and it may soon start to rain heavily.

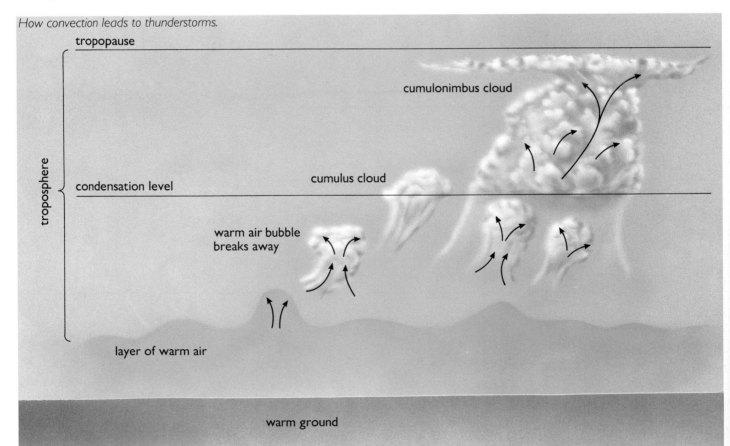

How convection leads to thunderstorms.

tropopause

troposphere

cumulonimbus cloud

condensation level

cumulus cloud

warm air bubble breaks away

layer of warm air

warm ground

THUNDERSTORMS

Thunderstorms are very large, intense, convectional showers. Concentrated heating of the ground in hot weather leads to powerful updraughts of air. These can rise as far as the tropopause, the limit of the lower atmosphere, 10,000m (over 30,000ft) above the Earth. At this height, the moisture in the air condenses into showers of ice and hail, which are buffeted up and down in the turbulence. Eventually the ice particles may melt into rain as they fall.

A lightning flash or thunderclap is the sign of a powerful electrical discharge. The lightning is seen before the thunder is heard, because light travels faster than sound. A thunderstorm is not just one storm, but a whole series of storm cells. As one cell dies away, new cells are being created, and it may be several hours before the storm dies altogether.

In temperate climates thunderstorms are most common in summer, and often bring to an end a period of hot, dry weather. In equatorial regions, however, they may occur every day as part of the normal weather pattern. The day starts off fine and dry, but by the afternoon an intense storm has set in which lasts until the evening. At any one time there are about 500 thunderstorms in the world, with 100 lightning strikes every second.

Right: *Lightning and thunder take place at the same time. A delay of three seconds between seeing the lightning and hearing the thunder means that the storm is about 1km (3,300ft) away.*

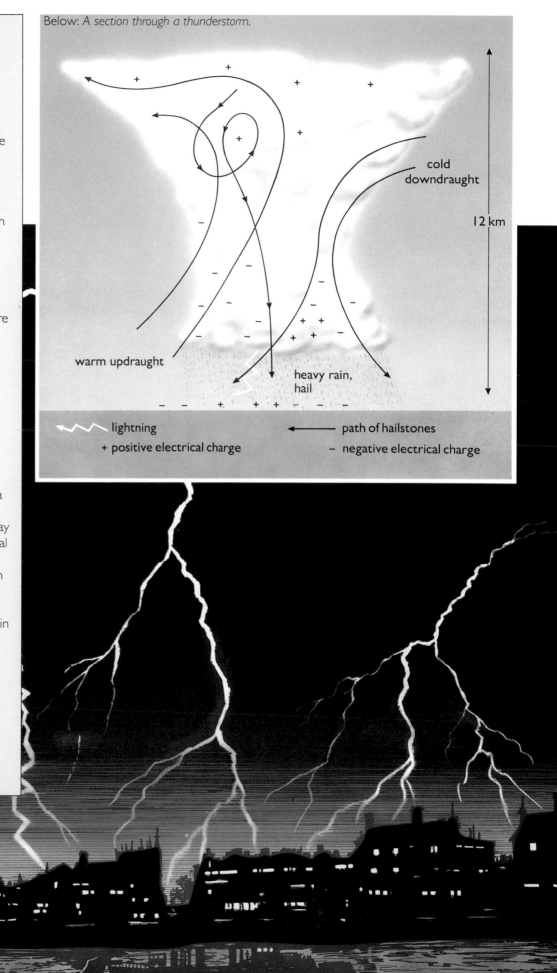

Below: *A section through a thunderstorm.*

cold downdraught

12 km

warm updraught

heavy rain, hail

lightning

+ positive electrical charge

path of hailstones

− negative electrical charge

Clouds and Rain

Clouds form when damp air cools, usually by rising. However, not all clouds bring rain. Some clouds warn of the possibility of rain in the near future, while others show that the weather will remain fine.

High, middle and low clouds
High clouds are found at between 6,000 and 12,000m (about 20,000–40,000ft).

Cirrus are clouds that are composed of microscopic ice crystals and look like wisps of hair or feathers. Cirrostratus – clouds that are also made of ice crystals – forms a whitish veil through which the Sun can just be seen as a bright halo. Cirrocumulus is similar, but more heaped and puffier. All these clouds indicate some turbulence in the upper atmosphere, but are too high to bring bad weather to lower cloud layers.

Clouds at heights between 1,500 and 6,000m (5,000–20,000ft) are of the altus type;

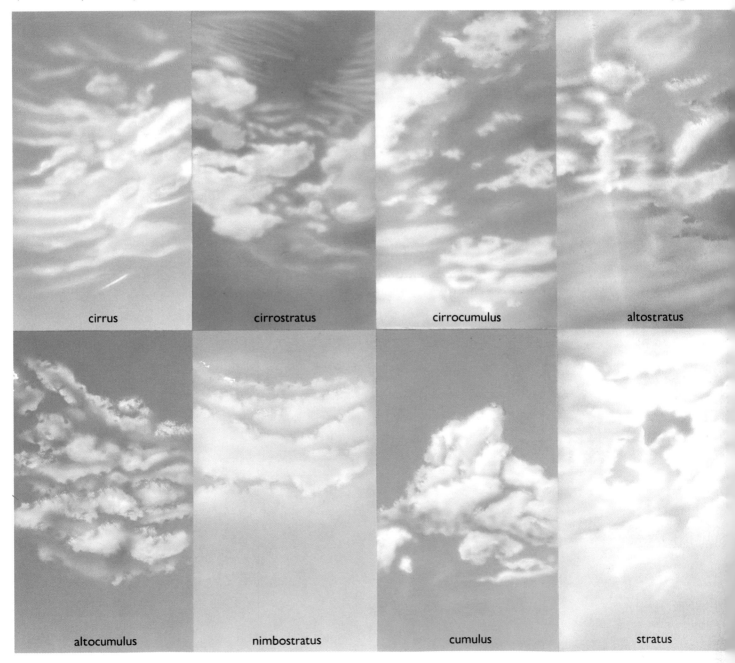

cirrus

cirrostratus

cirrocumulus

altostratus

altocumulus

nimbostratus

cumulus

stratus

that is, they often indicate that wet weather is on the way shortly, perhaps as the air is forced up along a front, a boundary between warm and cold air. Altostratus is a grey uniform sheet of cloud that might already be producing drizzle. Altocumulus is similar to cirrocumulus, but the patches are bigger, and often have a regular, fleecy appearance giving what is known as a 'mackerel sky'.

Low clouds are found at heights up to 1,500m (5,000ft). Stratus and nimbostratus form thick, grey layers, giving overcast skies for long periods. They often bring steady rain, perhaps temporarily clearing to allow the Sun to brighten up the sky for a short time.

Towering clouds

Some clouds extend through several layers of the atmosphere, gradually developing and towering upwards. Cumulus, which forms as a result of convection on a hot day, consists of numerous puffy, heaped clouds, which shine brilliant white in the Sun and have flat, dark bases. Often the cumulus drifts along without rising further, and there is little risk of rain.

Sometimes, however, the cumulus thickens up and grows into huge towering masses extending to great heights. This is cumulonimbus

TYPES OF RAIN

Convectional rain, which includes heavy showers and thunderstorms, is one of three main types. A second type, relief rain, occurs when a wind rises to cross hills or mountains. Most of the rain falls on the windward side of the hill. By the time the wind reaches the leeward (sheltered) side there is no cloud left. The leeward side is in what is known as a rain shadow.

Frontal rain occurs along a boundary, or front, between air at different temperatures. Warm air is forced above cold air, producing condensation, clouds and rain.

– clouds that bring intense storms and heavy rain. In a thunderstorm the top of the clouds spread out into a great anvil shape or nimbus, discharging masses of ice pellets and snow which reach the ground as large, cold raindrops.

Below: *How relief rain occurs.*

cumulonimbus

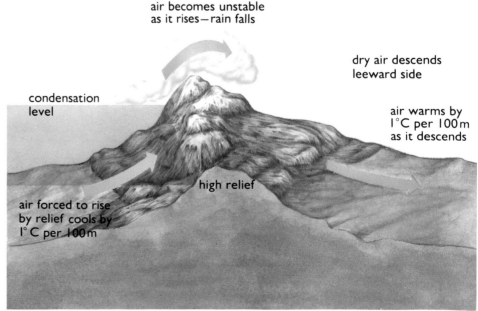

air becomes unstable as it rises—rain falls

dry air descends leeward side

condensation level

air warms by 1°C per 100m as it descends

high relief

air forced to rise by relief cools by 1°C per 100m

Anticyclones and Depressions

Weather forecasters often refer to 'anticyclones' and 'depressions'. Both are systems of circulating air produced by the combined effect of the Sun's heating of the Earth's surface and the Earth's rotation. In particular, they control whether the conditions that the winds bring us are dry and sunny, or wet and cloudy.

Anticyclones

Anticyclones are masses of dense, heavy air, shown on weather maps as high-pressure cells, or circular areas with 'high' written inside them. Anticyclones are often very large, sometimes covering entire continents. Spiralling winds blow out of them, twisting clockwise in the northern hemisphere, and anticlockwise in the southern hemisphere. Usually they start over land, because the winds blowing from them are often dry. Since the air is heavy it tends to prevent upward convectional currents from developing, and hence clouds and rain from forming.

Once an anticyclone, or 'high', sets in, it can bring dry weather for several weeks. 'Ridges of high pressure' are similar but smaller and weaker, and may last for only a few days. In summer anticyclones bring long, hot, dry spells – 'heatwave' weather. In winter, anticyclones bring cold, frosty days with clear skies.

A cross-section of a depression.

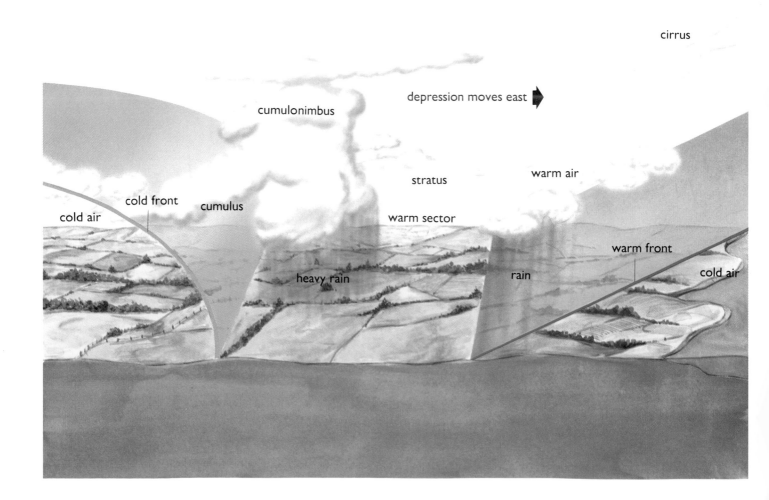

cirrus

depression moves east ▶

cumulonimbus

stratus

warm air

cold front

cumulus

warm sector

warm front

cold air

cold air

heavy rain

rain

cold air

Below: *How a depression develops.*

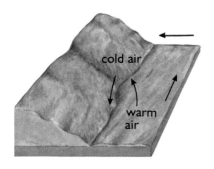

a. *A wave develops between the warm and cold air.*

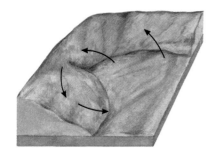

b. *The cold air pushes beneath the warm air, lifting it up.*

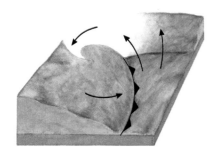

c. *Cold and warm fronts separate the two sorts of air.*

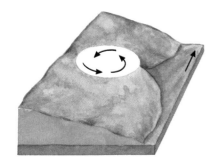

d. *The warm air is lifted up completely and occluded.*

Depressions

Storms caused by the mixing of different kinds of air are called depressions. In the northern hemisphere they begin over the Atlantic Ocean where warm, wet tropical winds meet colder air from polar regions. The turbulence between the two sorts of air creates a rotating storm of 'low pressure' in which the warmer air swirls up above the cold air.

The uplift produces condensation, clouds and rain, especially along the fronts or boundaries between the two air masses. The weather maps show fronts as lines extending outwards from the centre of the depression. Gradually, as the storm loses its energy, it dies away. A dying depression is said to be occluded.

Once depressions form, they move eastwards across the Atlantic, bringing rain and unsettled conditions to western Europe. The weather brought by a depression varies considerably – from overcast, breezy weather with a few light showers, to intense

storms with gales and several hours of rain. The weather forecaster is often unsure how severe a depression will be.

Sometimes entire chains of depressions can form, with one following on the other. They will bring variable weather, extending over several weeks, with periods of cloud and rain separated by 'ridges' of high pressure bringing short, sunny spells.

A MOVING DEPRESSION

As the depression approaches, the sky will gradually become more overcast, first with cirrus and later with altus and stratus cloud types. There will be rain or drizzle as the warm front passes. The temperature may rise noticeably because of the warmer air behind the warm front.

The cold front brings heavy rain, often with much cumulus or cumulonimbus cloud formed, as air is forced upwards along the steeply inclined cold front. Behind the cold front, colder air moves in, bringing showers and unsettled weather for a time. It may take between 12 and 24 hours for the entire depression to pass.

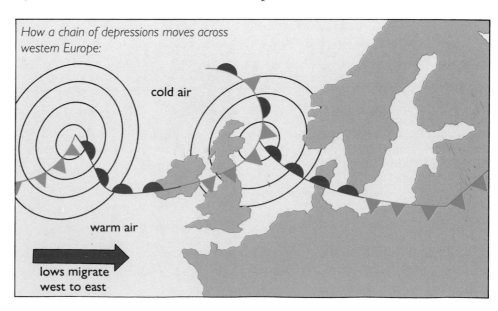

How a chain of depressions moves across western Europe:

cold air

warm air

lows migrate west to east

Weather in Towns

Towns and cities have a weather all of their own. Local weather forecasts have to take into account the distinctive atmospheric conditions that can develop over urban areas.

Heat islands

Towns and cities act rather like giant storage heaters. During the day, surfaces such as bricks, tarmac and concrete soak up the heat from the Sun. These surfaces are also heated from the inside by central heating and industrial activity. During the night this heat is gradually released, but the buildings can stay warm for a long time even though the temperature outside is falling. The dust and haze in the atmosphere reflects a lot of this heat back and prevents it from escaping.

As a result, towns and cities become 'heat islands', compared with the cooler surrounding countryside, and the bigger the city, the greater the heat island effect. The centres of large cities can be as much as 8–10°C warmer on a winter night than nearby rural areas. The heat island effects can sometimes be noticed even around a small group of buildings.

Yet although towns and cities are warmer than the countryside, they receive less sunshine on average. Cities are also rainier than other places, and very much foggier – they have about twice as much fog in winter compared with nearby rural places.

Urban climate

The wind speeds and wind directions given by the weather forecaster apply to open, unenclosed areas, but often not to towns and cities. Tall buildings such as offices and blocks of flats turn the open spaces, alleyways and passages between them into funnels that channel and concentrate air flows. This produces turbulence and eddying (a sort of whirlpool of air), turning parts of the city into gusty, unpleasant places in which to walk around.

Left: Towns and cities form 'heat islands' – especially on winter nights and in cold weather.

Below: As wind flows around buildings, it creates eddies and turbulence, leading to strong winds at ground level.

Cities and towns are some of the most polluted places to live in. During the day, factories send out smoke and poisonous gases, such as sulphur dioxide, which are added to by the exhausts from the thousands of motor vehicles that clog the city centres. If there is not enough wind to blow the pollutants away, they can build up into a large mass of photochemical smog, which covers the city. In many cities the concentration of poisonous gases in the air is as much as 200 times greater than normal. In some cities – for example Tokyo and Los Angeles – air pollution is so bad that regular readings are given on television, and special measures are taken when levels become too high.

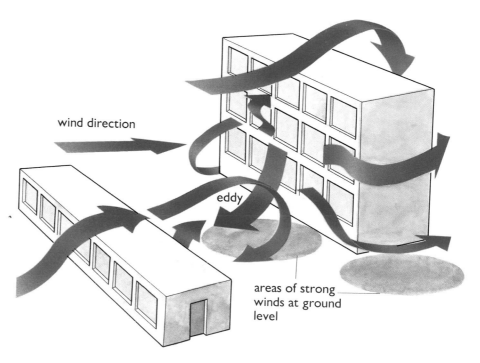

wind direction

eddy

areas of strong winds at ground level

Weather Hazards

Even the most carefully made plans can be ruined by the weather. Flights to holiday destinations are sometimes delayed by fog, and a holiday in search of the sun may end up being spoiled by rain. In some parts of the world weather hazards are so much a part of the way of life that the people have grown used to seeing damage to property and even loss of life as a result.

Fog

Fog consists of water vapour which has condensed, through cooling, to form tiny water droplets in the air. This can happen when the ground loses heat rapidly at night, cooling the layers of air above it. In urban areas the fog is made worse by dirt and poisonous gases released into the atmosphere from factory chimneys and car exhaust pipes. These gases turn the fog into a 'smog', which is a serious hazard to health. Fog can also occur when warm moist air is cooled as it passes over a cold land or sea surface.

Fog is declared when visibility falls below 1km (0.6 mile). Thick fog is a hazard to travelling, and is a frequent cause of motorway pile-ups – accidents involving many vehicles. It has also been

A tornado, or 'twister', on the Great Plains in the United States.

responsible for many aircraft disasters. In 1977 547 people were killed at Tenerife in the Canary Islands when two Boeing 747 jet airliners collided with each other on the runway in misty conditions.

Tornadoes

Tornadoes are very severe rotating storms. They happen when warm, moist air becomes trapped by cold, dry, thundery air above it. As the warm air rises, instead of mixing with the cold air it forms a violent upward spinning mass. A tornado is instantly recognized by the funnel of cloud which descends towards the ground.

Tornadoes are most common in the United States, which has about 1,000 of them every year. Wind speeds reach 350km/h (220mph) in the centre of the

Fog on motorways can cause multiple collisions involving scores of vehicles.

tornado, which can pick up buildings, livestock and people. The very low pressure at the core of the tornado can even cause buildings to explode. A tornado rarely lasts more than an hour, and is effective over a fairly small area. Some tornadoes measure only a few metres across. While it is possible to warn when a tornado is likely to develop, its path is very unpredictable.

Hurricanes and typhoons

Hurricanes (called typhoons and cyclones in the Pacific and Asia) are much bigger and far more damaging than tornadoes. They begin over warm, tropical seas in the Caribbean and in the Indian and Pacific Oceans. Heavy storm clouds are drawn into a swirling pattern of movement by the rotation of the Earth. Within the storm, masses of warm, moist air are pulled upwards to form dense thunderclouds, while in the centre, rotating winds can reach up to 270km/h (170mph).

Hurricanes can last for up to three weeks. During this time they can easily cover thousands of kilometres, devastating everything in their path. Some of the worst damage is done by storm surges. These are bulges in the ocean surface caused by the high winds. When they strike land, they can flatten coastal towns and villages and flood vast areas.

Once the hurricane strikes land, it begins to lose its force because it has no more warm water to provide its energy. Some poor countries like Bangladesh suffer heavily from typhoons. Bangladesh lies in the path of regular typhoon tracks but cannot afford the flood protection measures it needs. In 1991, about 250,000 people were killed when the worst cyclone this century destroyed the coastal lands of Bangladesh.

Above: *The swirling cloud patterns indicating a hurricane can be clearly seen from space.*

Below: *Areas of the world affected by hurricanes and typhoons.*

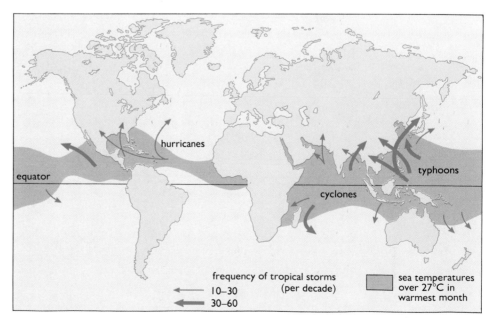

World Climate

Studies of the weather mostly concern short-term changes in conditions – for example, from one day to the next. Studies of climate are more to do with the general weather pattern over a year, or over several years. Climatic 'regions' are areas that share the same sort of climate. The same climatic region may be found in several parts of the world.

CLIMATIC TYPE	SAMPLE PLACE	HIGHEST MONTHLY TEMP (°C)	LOWEST MONTHLY TFMP (°C)	RAINFALL TOTAL (mm)
Polar,				
Sub-polar	Verkhoyansk, Russia	14	-50	134
Middle latitude,				
Maritime	Inverness, UK	14	3	729
Continental	Chicago, USA	23	-4	836
Sub-tropical,				
Humid	Hong Kong, Asia	28	15	2,162
Wet and dry	Athens, Greece	28	10	402
Tropical,				
Humid	Manaus, Brazil	29	27	1,811
Wet and dry	Lusaka, Zambia	24	16	836
Arid	Bahrain	34	17	81
Mountain	Quito, Ecuador	15	14	1,115

Polar and sub-polar climates

The 'Arctic' climatic region consists entirely of ice-caps and large areas covered permanently with ice and snow. These areas have long winter days. Some places within the Arctic Circle experience several days in December when there is no daylight at all. Sub-polar regions are just warm enough in the brief summer to support a tundra vegetation of mosses and short flowering plants.

Middle latitude climates

Middle latitude, or temperate climates are of two types. The maritime type, which is found in, for example, western Europe, gives cool summers and mild winters. Winter temperatures are maintained by the Gulf Stream, which moves warm water into the north Atlantic. Central and eastern Europe do not feel the effects of the Gulf Stream and so have a more extreme, or continental type of climate,

with much cooler winters. Much of North America has a continental climate.

Sub-tropical and tropical climates

Climates experiencing hot summers and mild winters outside the tropics are said to be sub-tropical. The humid type has rain in most months of the year; the Mediterranean type has a distinctive winter rainfall maximum and a summer drought. The

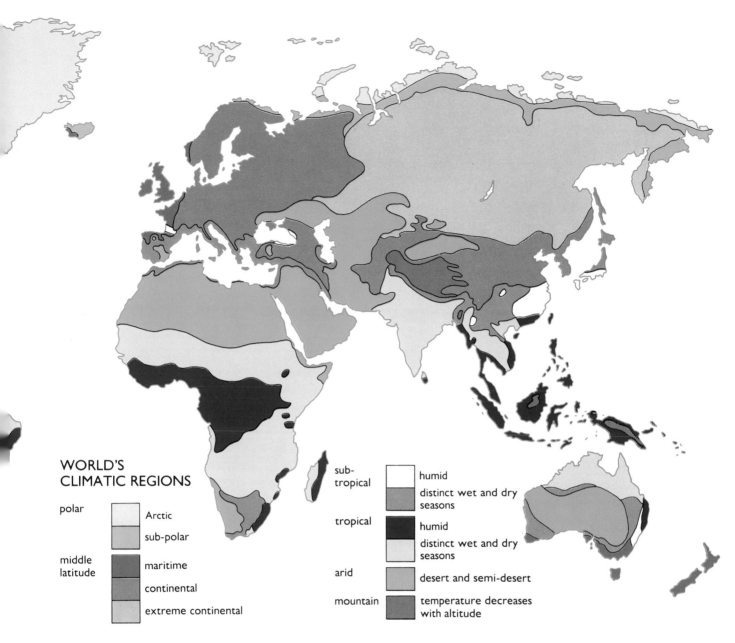

WORLD'S
CLIMATIC REGIONS

polar
- Arctic
- sub-polar

middle
latitude
- maritime
- continental
- extreme continental

sub-
tropical
- humid
- distinct wet and dry seasons

tropical
- humid
- distinct wet and dry seasons

arid
- desert and semi-desert

mountain
- temperature decreases with altitude

Mediterranean type is shared by most countries bordering the Mediterranean Sea, as well as by some other areas of the world.

Many places close to the equator have a humid or equatorial type of climate. The weather is consistently hot and wet, with little seasonal variation, and with rain falling on most days of the year.

Further from the equator, the climate within the tropics of Cancer and Capricorn is of the 'wet and dry' type, with a rainy summer and dry winter. In eastern and southern Asia the summers are particularly wet because of the heavy monsoon rains.

Arid climates

Desert and semi-desert areas receive less rainfall than elsewhere and have an arid, or dry climate. In tropical deserts rainless winds keep the sky clear of clouds, so that the ground heats up to some of the world's highest temperatures. Patagonia, in South America, and the Gobi of central Asia are temperate or cold deserts, with a lower range of temperatures than the tropical deserts.

Mountain climates

In mountainous areas altitude has the effect of reducing temperatures. In most other respects, however, these areas have the same climate as regions around them.

Changing Climates

Climates have changed throughout the Earth's history. The fossils of dinosaurs found in areas that are now deserts show that at one time, these places had humid climates. Even during the short time that humans have been on Earth the climate has changed considerably. People today, however, are themselves partly responsible for climatic change.

Climates of the past

Until about 10,000 years ago large areas of Britain, Europe and North America were covered by ice. The ice gradually retreated to produce first a tundra and then the temperate climate of today. Within this general warming there have been shorter warm and cold phases. The Middle Ages seem to have been a relatively warm period. Vineyards flourished in parts of southern Britain where it would be too cold to grow grapes today. Viking settlers colonized and grew crops in Greenland, in areas where this would now be impossible.

Between the 16th and 19th centuries the climate of Europe became colder again. Rivers and canals regularly froze in winter, and mountain glaciers extended further down valleys than they do today. Fairs and ice games on the River Thames were popular, and were not regarded as unsafe, because the river was so solidly frozen over.

What causes climatic change?

A change in climate can have a number of causes. According to the Milankovitch theory, it occurs when the position of the Earth on its axis changes. This in turn affects the distance of the Earth's surface from the Sun, making it colder when the surface is farther away. Other possible causes include the dust from volcanic eruptions, which absorbs sunlight, and the occurrence of sunspots on the Sun's surface, which produces variations in the Sun's heat output.

During the last 100 years, average global temperature has risen by about 0.5°C. This might not seem much, but even small changes in average global temperatures can cause major changes in climatic patterns. Some scientists think that in the long term, this general warming may be coming to an end, and that another Ice Age might start in about 5,000 years' time.

The 'greenhouse' effect

In the near future, the climate is likely to get warmer still. This is because human activity is adding an increasing quantity of gases to the atmosphere, especially carbon dioxide, methane and nitrous oxide. These are called greenhouse gases because they act like the windows of a greenhouse. They allow incoming solar radiation to pass through them, but prevent outgoing heat from escaping. The burning of tropical forests, mainly to provide cattle pastures, and of fossil fuels (coal and oil) in industry and power stations, are largely responsible for the increase. Another problem,

People skating on the frozen River Thames in London.

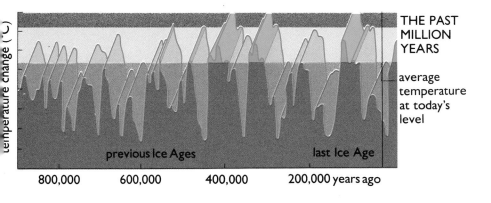

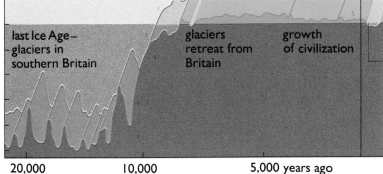

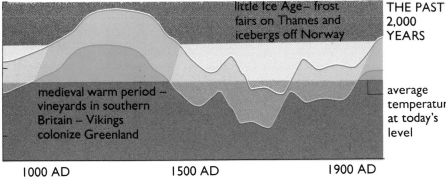

How climate has varied in recent geological time.

which has only recently come to light, is the thinning of the ozone layer of the atmosphere. The ozone layer protects the Earth from excessive ultraviolet radiation, and its destruction is further contributing to global warming. One of the causes has been identified as the use of chlorofluorocarbons (CFCs) found in aerosols and refrigerators.

A new climatic map
Scientists have worked out that a doubling of the amount of atmospheric carbon dioxide might increase temperatures over northern Europe and North America by as much as 8°C. This would greatly alter the map of world climatic regions. Places now shown as middle latitudes would become sub-tropical, and would be able to grow a greater range of crops. But many drier tropical areas would experience constant drought, and famines on a massive scale would result.

Another worry is that global warming might melt the ice-caps, causing sea-levels to rise and many coastal cities to be flooded. Not surprisingly, the greenhouse effect is now seen as one of the world's major environmental problems.

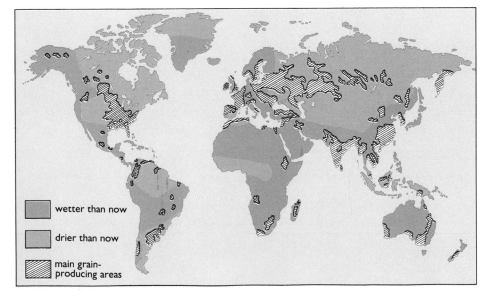

Many of the world's main grain-producing areas lie in parts of the world which would become drier with global warming.

References

Air pressure The force or weight of air over a certain area, measured in millibars (mb). Pressure is measured with a barometer.

Altus A cloud of middle altitudes. Altocumulus (heaped) and altostratus (layered) are the main types.

Anemometer An instrument with rotating cups for measuring wind speed.

Anticyclone A system of winds rotating outwards from a mass of air at high pressure. Anticyclones usually bring dry weather.

Beaufort scale A scale for measuring wind speed. It ranges from Force 0 to Force 12 (hurricane force).

Cirrus A cloud of high altitudes, consisting of ice crystals. Cirrostratus (layered) and cirrocumulus (heaped) are the main types.

Condensation The change in water, on cooling, from water vapour into liquid droplets.

Continental climate A climate which occurs in the interiors of large continents. It has warm or hot summers and cold winters.

Convection Heating of the air by the Sun, producing rising currents of warm air. Convection of damp air may lead to condensation, clouds and rain.

Cumulus A heaped cloud formed by convection.

Cyclone A system of winds rotating inwards to an area of low pressure. Depressions, tornadoes and hurricanes (typhoons) are all cyclones.

Depression A type of cyclone common in many temperate parts of the world. It normally has warm and cold fronts, separating air at different temperatures.

Equatorial climate A climate characterized by heavy rainfall and high temperatures all year.

Fog A thick mist formed from the condensation of water vapour through cooling of the air.

Front A boundary between warm and cold air. *See* **Depression.**

Frost A white coating formed by the condensation of water droplets as ice on surfaces such as grass and windows.

Greenhouse effect (global warming) The warming up of the atmosphere as a result of increasing concentrations of carbon dioxide and other greenhouse gases. It may cause widespread climatic change in the foreseeable future.

Hail Small pieces of ice which form within a cloud by the build-up of freezing water around a particle of dust.

Heat island The effect built-up areas have in raising the temperature of the air around them.

Hurricane A tropical revolving storm, known as a cyclone or typhoon in the Asiatic and Pacific areas, and as a willy-willy in Australia. Hurricanes have rotating patterns of violent winds.

Isobar A line on a weather map joining points of equal atmospheric pressure.

Maritime climate A type of climate influenced by the sea. It has cool summers and mild winters.

Mediterranean climate A sub-tropical climate with warm, dry summers and mild, damp winters. It is also found in California and South Africa.

Meteosat A satellite which transmits pictures of the weather to Earth. Meteosat is positioned over the equator to 'see' Africa, Europe and western Asia.

Milankovitch theory The theory that shifts in the position of the Earth on its axis can influence the amount of solar heating received at the Earth's surface.

Occlusion The end-stage in the life of a depression. The warm air is lifted entirely above the cold air as pressure rises, and the system of fronts soon disappears. *See also* **Depression.**

Ozone layer A layer of ozone gas which surrounds the Earth at high altitude and protects the surface from excessive ultra-violet radiation from the Sun. Scientists are concerned that the ozone layer has become thinner in recent years.

Photochemical smog A polluted fog formed by the action of sunlight on poisonous gases and particles such as nitrogen oxides and hydrocarbons. The pollutants are produced by vehicle and industrial emissions.

Precipitation Moisture from the sky falling as rain, snow, sleet or hail.

Rain shadow The sheltered, leeward side of a hill which remains dry from relief rain.

Relief rain Rain produced where damp air is forced over a range of hills or mountains.

Ridge of high pressure A region on a weather map that sometimes separates two areas of low pressure.

Run-off Rainwater that flows on the surface and eventually reaches rivers or streams.

Snow Tiny ice crystals formed from frozen water vapour.

Synoptic chart A large map or chart summarizing all the information that is known about the weather.

Thunderstorm An intense convectional shower. One storm may consist of numerous thunder cells forming and dying throughout the storm. Electrical discharges produce thunder and lightning. The storm is about 1km (0.6 mile) away for every three seconds of delay between the lightning and the thunder.

Tornado A small, violent rotating storm. Tornadoes, or twisters, are common in the central and eastern United States. They follow a narrow path and die away after about an hour.

Typhoon A tropical revolving storm found in Asia and the Pacific. *See* **Hurricane.**

Our Environment

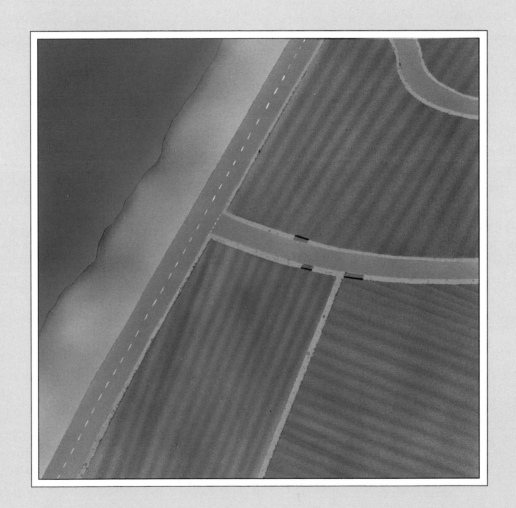

The Water Cycle

The basis of life on Earth is water. At any one time there is about 1,384 million cubic kilometres (331 million cubic miles) of it, by far the greatest part making up the oceans and seas. The rest is fresh water, of which 90 per cent is in Antarctica, where it contributes little to sustaining life. The remaining 10 per cent circulates within the atmosphere, through river and lake systems, through the soil or rocks, and through plant and animal tissues.

The hydrological cycle

The circulation of water through the Earth's natural systems is known as the hydrological cycle. Within the cycle there are numerous 'stores' where water is retained, sometimes for long periods – for instance, within lakes or the oceans, or in rocks underground. The water moves between stores as 'flows' – such as river movements – or the rising of water vapour through convection in the atmosphere to form clouds. The Sun provides the energy for convection, whereas the energy for rivers and running water comes from gravity.

Solar heating produces evaporation of moisture as water vapour. Enormous quantities of water from the oceans are evaporated, especially in hot, tropical areas, but evaporation also occurs from the surfaces of ponds, lakes, rivers and puddles. As the water vapour rises, it cools and condenses to form clouds, which may be blown some distance before falling as rain.

Water in plants and the soil

Not all rain reaches the ground. Some of it is caught by the leaves and branches of trees and plants. This may drip down the leaf stem and eventually reach the ground, or it may stay on the leaf surface, and evaporate back into the atmosphere later.

Some of the moisture percolates or 'infiltrates' into the soil. This is picked up by the roots of growing plants, and after rising through the plant tissue 'transpires' back into the atmosphere from the plant leaves. This is a form of evaporation.

Above and below ground

On and below the ground, the rain can follow a number of routes. In areas with steep slopes and bare rock surfaces, some rainwater runs straight off the surface and down the hillside. Other water may percolate through the soil layers and seep out to the surface at the bottoms of slopes. Water that sinks further down into the underlying permeable rocks (rocks able to hold water) is called groundwater. This may reach the surface again through a spring. The water from run-off, seepage and springs collects in gullies, which join together to form a branching river network – the last stage in the hydrological cycle, before the water returns to the sea.

DISTRIBUTION OF THE EARTH'S WATER

lakes, rivers and atmosphere 0.02%

underground aquifers 0.61%

ice-caps and glaciers 2.09%

oceans and seas 97.29%

Most of the Earth's water is in the oceans and seas. Only a tiny part is circulating through the remaining stores in the hydrological cycle.

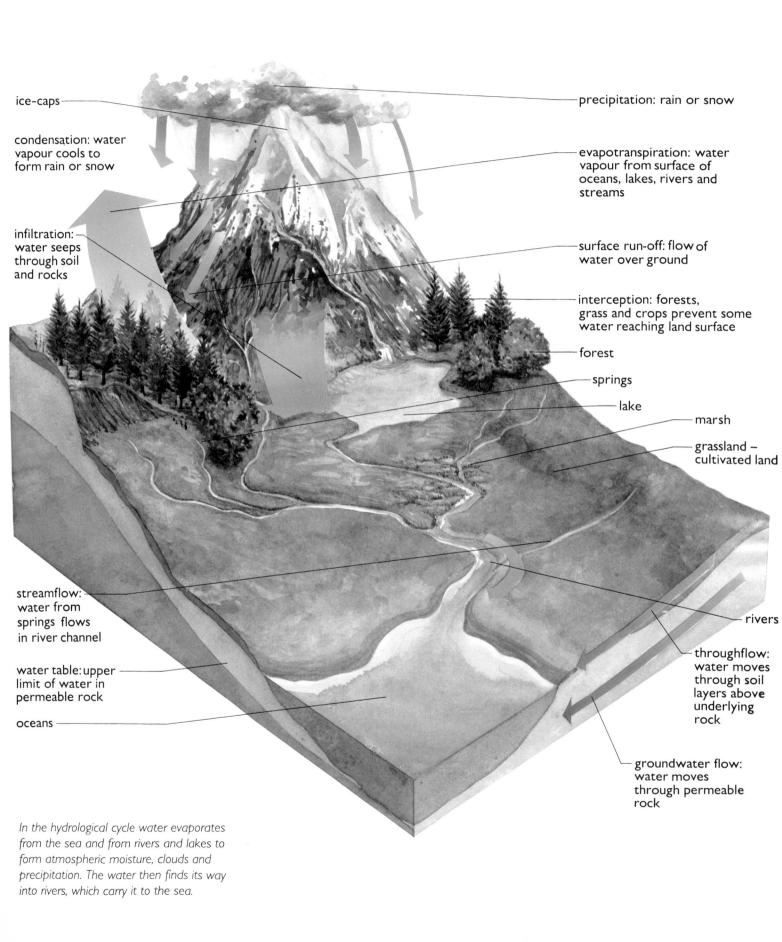

ice-caps

precipitation: rain or snow

condensation: water vapour cools to form rain or snow

evapotranspiration: water vapour from surface of oceans, lakes, rivers and streams

infiltration: water seeps through soil and rocks

surface run-off: flow of water over ground

interception: forests, grass and crops prevent some water reaching land surface

forest

springs

lake

marsh

grassland – cultivated land

streamflow: water from springs flows in river channel

water table: upper limit of water in permeable rock

oceans

rivers

throughflow: water moves through soil layers above underlying rock

groundwater flow: water moves through permeable rock

In the hydrological cycle water evaporates from the sea and from rivers and lakes to form atmospheric moisture, clouds and precipitation. The water then finds its way into rivers, which carry it to the sea.

The Soil

The soil is the Earth's most valuable resource. Although in places it is less than 1m (3.3ft) deep, without it there would be no human or animal life. Soil is rich in organisms. It is estimated that a handful of good-quality soil has a more complex biological structure than the whole of the surface of Jupiter. Yet, despite its importance, soil throughout the world is being eroded at an alarming rate.

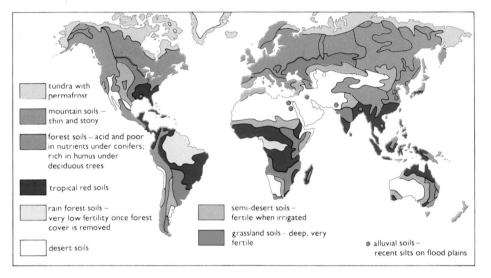

tundra with permafrost

mountain soils – thin and stony

forest soils – acid and poor in nutrients under conifers; rich in humus under deciduous trees

tropical red soils

rain forest soils – very low fertility once forest cover is removed

desert soils

semi-desert soils – fertile when irrigated

grassland soils – deep, very fertile

alluvial soils – recent silts on flood plains

The world's main soil groups. Within these groups there are many variations in soil type. Soils can vary even within a very small area.

How is soil formed?

The greater part of the soil's weight comes from weathered rock material. Any sample of soil contains a range of grains of different sizes, varying from sand (the coarsest), to silt and clay (the finest). The texture of the soil is said to be sandy or clayey depending on the mix of grain sizes.

The organic life in the soil comes from rotting vegetation and dead or decaying animal matter. As organic material decays, it is converted into humus. This may account for as little as one per cent of the soil's weight, but it is the vital element which provides the nutrients needed by growing plants. The soil itself is teeming with life. A mere 30g (1oz) of fertile soil contains a million bacteria of just one type, while 1 hectare (2.4 acres) may contain up to 300 million small invertebrates such as millipedes, other insects and worms.

What makes a fertile soil?

The most suitable soil for cultivating crops is a loam. This is a soil with a balanced mixture of sandy, silty and clayey particles. The loam retains moisture but is well drained, so that plant roots can easily penetrate the soil to obtain the nutrients they need.

Soil fertility also depends on processes within the soil itself. In wet areas, rainwater tends to wash many of the nutrients out of the soil. Known as leaching, this leads to the soil becoming more acidic. In dry areas moisture is drawn up to the surface where it evaporates, leaving behind a crust of salts which make the soil unfit for cultivation. Constant cropping also

Some soil conservation measures.

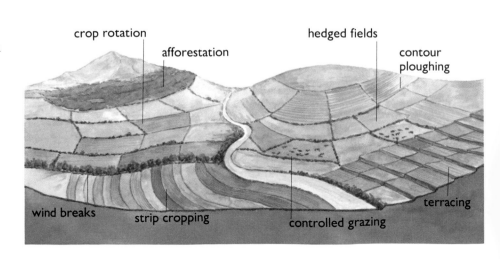

crop rotation

afforestation

hedged fields

contour ploughing

wind breaks

strip cropping

controlled grazing

terracing

deprives the soil of nutrients, so that gradually its fertility declines.

Food growers have to look after the soil carefully if it is to remain fertile. Plant foods must be replenished by adding fertilizers or organic composts, and acidity may have to be countered by adding lime from time to time.

Soil erosion

The quantity of soil on the Earth's surface is diminishing. Although it takes several centuries for a new layer of soil 1cm (0.4in) thick to form, soil is being eroded all over the world at many times this rate. Each year, soil erosion helps to make 11 million hectares (26.4 million acres) of land uncultivable.

Soil can be blown away by the wind or washed down a slope by surface run-off. Soil erosion is rare on vegetated or cultivated land, because the plants bind the soil particles together and give protection from the wind and rain, but it readily takes place on bare land. In temperate countries the large open fields required for intensive crop farming are vulnerable to wind erosion if left bare for a long period. In tropical lands, clearance of rain forests is a cause of soil erosion, for once the trees have been cleared there is nothing to protect the land from the heavy tropical rains. Although measures to prevent erosion are possible, losses from soil erosion worldwide are increasing.

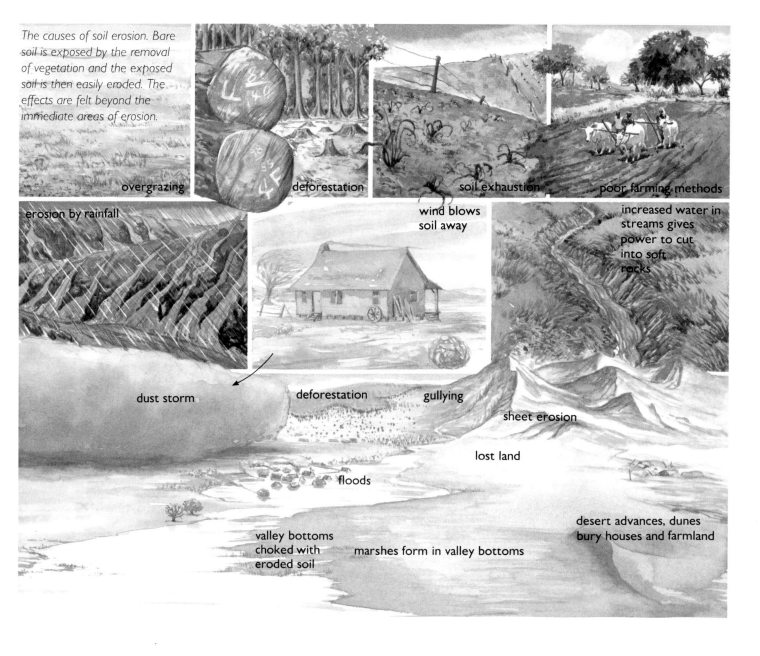

The causes of soil erosion. Bare soil is exposed by the removal of vegetation and the exposed soil is then easily eroded. The effects are felt beyond the immediate areas of erosion.

overgrazing

deforestation

soil exhaustion

poor farming methods

erosion by rainfall

wind blows soil away

increased water in streams gives power to cut into soft rocks

dust storm

deforestation

gullying

sheet erosion

lost land

floods

valley bottoms choked with eroded soil

marshes form in valley bottoms

desert advances, dunes bury houses and farmland

The Green Mantle

The Earth's vegetation cover, or 'green mantle', contains well over 300,000 plant species. Vegetation is linked to animal life in natural systems, called ecosystems, and forms part of the 'food chain' on which all animal life depends. It has been estimated that the loss of one plant species can lead to the eventual extinction of up to 30 animal species as the consequences are passed along the food chain.

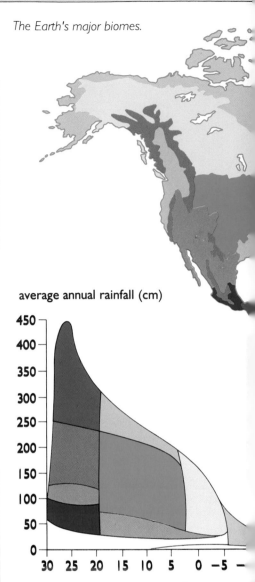

The Earth's major biomes.

Vegetation succession

Trees and other tall plants are the result of vegetation succession – a long series of plant developments. The first plants to appear are those such as mosses and lichens which can grow on a bare rock surface without soil. When these die they decay, and their remains rot to form a basic soil, perhaps enough for the seeds of rough grasses to take hold. The roots of the grasses penetrate into cracks and joints in the rock, opening them up and making it easier for the roots of other plants to become established.

The soil eventually becomes deep enough to hold the roots of tall plants such as ferns or shrubs. These cast a shadow which keeps the sunlight off the mosses and grasses, and so they cease to spread. The shrubs, in turn, become overshadowed by the branches of tall-growing trees, which can now take root in the deep, fertile soil formed from the decay of other vegetation.

In this way the vegetation succession leads to the community of plants becoming dominated by trees. But for this to happen there must be

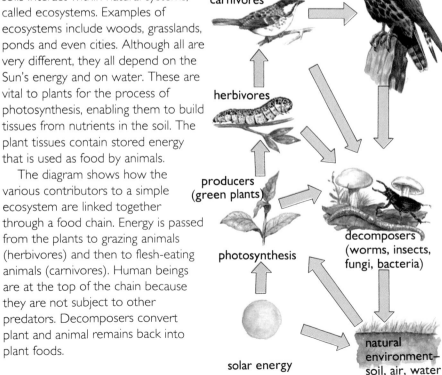

ECOSYSTEMS

Plants, animals, people, climate and soils interact within natural systems, called ecosystems. Examples of ecosystems include woods, grasslands, ponds and even cities. Although all are very different, they all depend on the Sun's energy and on water. These are vital to plants for the process of photosynthesis, enabling them to build tissues from nutrients in the soil. The plant tissues contain stored energy that is used as food by animals.

The diagram shows how the various contributors to a simple ecosystem are linked together through a food chain. Energy is passed from the plants to grazing animals (herbivores) and then to flesh-eating animals (carnivores). Human beings are at the top of the chain because they are not subject to other predators. Decomposers convert plant and animal remains back into plant foods.

top carnivores

carnivores

herbivores

producers (green plants)

photosynthesis

decomposers (worms, insects, fungi, bacteria)

solar energy

natural environment– soil, air, water

average annual rainfall (cm)

450
400
350
300
250
200
150
100
50
0

30 25 20 15 10 5 0 −5 −

average annual temperatu

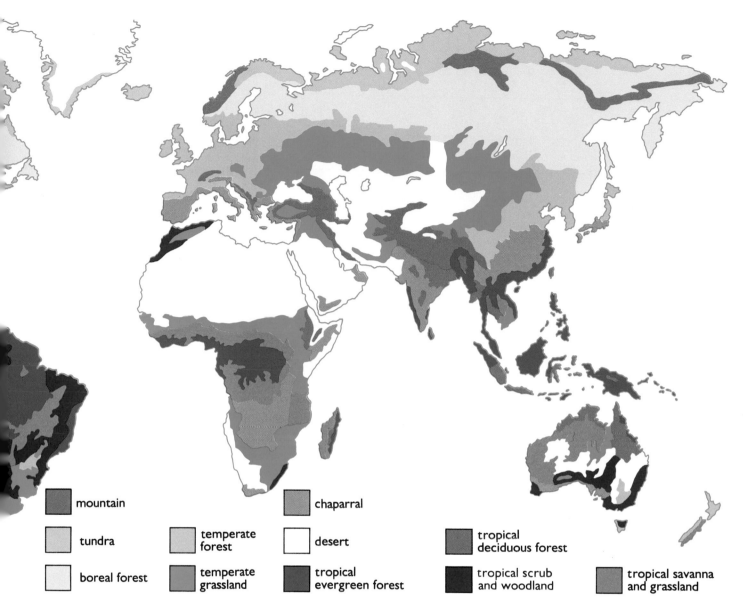

mountain

tundra

boreal forest

temperate forest

temperate grassland

chaparral

desert

tropical evergreen forest

tropical deciduous forest

tropical scrub and woodland

tropical savanna and grassland

plenty of moisture and sunlight. Moreover, there must be little or no interference from people and their domestic grazing animals, which tend to chew the growing roots and prevent plants from growing up again.

Major biomes

A biome is a community of plants and animals extending over a large natural area. Some 10 major biomes have been identified worldwide. The character of a biome depends on temperature and rainfall conditions. Biomes determine the character of the soil beneath them. The most productive biomes are the tropical forests, which account for one-third of the Earth's total biomass (organic material) even though they occupy only ten per cent of the land area. By contrast, deserts and tundras produce only two per cent, yet they cover a quarter of the land surfaces.

All biomes have been affected by human activity, particularly forests that have been cleared for cultivation.

It is possible to predict what the likely biome will be for anywhere on the Earth provided that the temperature and rainfall conditions are known. However, the diagram is only very generalized and does not take account of relief and soil, which also help to determine vegetation.

Temperate forest now hardly exists in Europe and North America as a result of human interference. It is feared likely that much of the natural tropical evergreen forest will also have vanished entirely by the end of this century.

Forests

Forests cover 30 per cent of the Earth's land surface. They yield more biomass and contain more species than any other biome. They also play a major role by recycling carbon dioxide back into oxygen, and so help to control global temperature by limiting the greenhouse effect. They protect soil from erosion, supply the fuel needs of half the world's people, and provide wood for paper pulp and timber.

Boreal forest

Boreal forest, or taiga, is the forest of the colder areas of the northern continents at latitudes of between about 50–55 and 65. It also covers the slopes of major mountain ranges, particularly the Himalayas, Rockies and Andes. Boreal forest consists mostly of conifers, evergreen needle-bearing trees such as pine, fir and spruce. The conifer needles prevent loss of moisture by transpiration during the winter months, when rainfall is low and most moisture is frozen into the ground. A few broad-leaved trees such as birch, alder or willow survive the cold conditions.

Temperate forest

Temperate forest occurs between latitudes 40 and 65 in areas where there is sufficient moisture to support forest growth. This forest is varied and includes both evergreen coniferous and deciduous trees, which shed their leaves in winter. Deciduous forest dominates in areas where all-year rain ensures a continuous supply of moisture. Beech, chestnut, oak, birch, alder, hornbeam, hazel, maple, hickory, ash, walnut and elm are common deciduous trees.

The conifers in temperate forests include the wellingtonia, a native of California, which grows to over 80m (260ft) and may live for up to 4,000 years. Another conifer, the redwood, can reach 112m (370ft).

The tropical rain forests by the end of the century will be only a fraction of their present size.

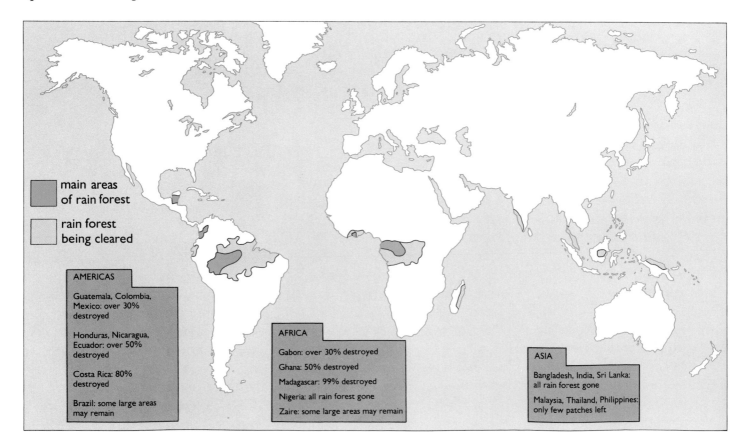

main areas
of rain forest

rain forest
being cleared

AMERICAS

Guatemala, Colombia,
Mexico: over 30%
destroyed

Honduras, Nicaragua,
Ecuador: over 50%
destroyed

Costa Rica: 80%
destroyed

Brazil: some large areas
may remain

AFRICA

Gabon: over 30% destroyed

Ghana: 50% destroyed

Madagascar: 99% destroyed

Nigeria: all rain forest gone

Zaire: some large areas may remain

ASIA

Bangladesh, India, Sri Lanka:
all rain forest gone

Malaysia, Thailand, Philippines:
only few patches left

THE PRODUCTS AND BENEFITS
OF TROPICAL FORESTS

Industrial and commercial
Gums, resins, oil.
Hardwood for furniture.
Timber.
Veneers.
Pulpwood.
Spices.
Drugs, herbs for medicinal use.

Ecological benefits
Conversion of carbon dioxide into
    oxygen.
Diversity of species.

Local uses
Food from plants.
Weaving materials.
Fuel and charcoal.
Soil for agriculture.
Drugs for illnesses.
Silkworms, bee keeping.
Building materials.

Tropical forest

Tropical rain forest, or selva, is the natural vegetation of tropical areas with all-year rainfall. About 60 per cent of the selva is in Central and South America; most of the remainder is in Central Africa and in South-east Asia. In these areas temperatures are high throughout the year, with little seasonal variation, and there is heavy rain in most months. Without seasons the forest is continually growing, dying and being renewed.

Boreal forest is mostly conifers. Temperate forests are a mix of conifers and deciduous trees. Tropical forests are evergreen, with new trees growing up as others decay.

boreal forest (taiga)

temperate forest

tropical forest

Tropical forests are valued for their hardwoods such as mahogany. The trees form a dense canopy up to 60m (200ft) in height which prevents light from reaching the forest floor and shades out lower growing trees and shrubs. Besides timber, the rain forests provide a huge number of other commodities. It has been said that each time we read a book, drive a car, drink coffee or take a pill we are using something from the tropical rain forest.

Vanishing forests

The world's forests are retreating. In the developed countries most of the natural forest disappeared long ago as land was cleared for cultivation. Some of the forests were replaced by planted woodlands, but the rate of planting does not keep pace with people's demands for timber products. The world now uses enough wood each year to cover a city the size of Birmingham to the height of a 10-storey building.

The tropical rain forests are vanishing at an alarming rate. One cause is the demand for tropical hardwoods, especially from the United States and Japan. In Brazil and Central America thousands of square kilometres of forest have been felled to provide new land for homeless peasants and cattle ranchers. The destruction is considered to be a major world environmental problem, for it could alter the amount of carbon dioxide in the atmosphere and hence the entire world climate.

Grasslands

Grasslands are the natural environment in many parts of the world where it is too dry for forests. Along its wetter margins the grassland gradually merges into forest, whereas along drier margins it becomes intermingled with scrub and then desert. How high the grassland grows depends on the rainfall.

CHANGES IN RAINFALL AND VEGETATION ACROSS WEST AFRICA

	Agades (17°)	Kano (12°30')		Port Harcourt (4°40')
Latitude (°N)	20	15	10	5
Rainfall totals	under 250mm		750mm	2,000mm
Rainfall reliability	very unreliable		fairly unreliable	reliable
Length of rainy season (months)	1–2			10–12
Vegetation	desert types	short grass	long grass scattered trees	rain forest coastal mangrove forest

Below: *Herdsmen from the savanna belts of West Africa.*

Tropical grassland

Tropical grasslands, or savannas, are found in tropical areas where rainfall is too seasonal for the growth of forest. They are mostly to the north and to the south of the rain forest belts in South America and Africa. There are also extensive savannas elsewhere, such as in the

SAVANNA IN WEST AFRICA

The table left and map below show the changes that occur along a line, or transect, from Port Harcourt in Nigeria to Agades in Niger. Port Harcourt is on the Niger delta, a large area of mangrove swamps, sandy beaches and lagoons. Northwards the line passes through an east–west zone of rain forest, where the climate is hot, wet and humid all the year round.

Northwards the forest thins into open woodland and savanna as total rainfall declines and the rainy season becomes shorter. In the dry upland plateau lands of Niger around Kano, the rainfall is only a fraction of the coastal total, and there is a marked dry season between November and March. These are the lands of the Fulani and Hausa peoples who live by rearing cattle.

Further north again, the savannas pass into semi-desert around Agades, before the grasslands give way to the dry scrub of the desert margins.

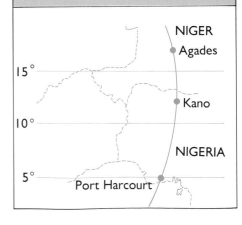

Deccan region of India, and in northern Australia.

In all these areas a summer rainy season promotes the rapid growth of vegetation for a short time, but this quickly withers during the remaining dry parts of the year. The tallest grasses, called elephant grass, can grow up to 5m (16ft), but in the drier areas grasses are much shorter. The expanses of grass are broken by clumps of trees which never grow very tall and have thick stems for storing water during the dry season.

Temperate grasslands

In temperate areas, the grasslands are typical of continental interiors far from coastal rain-bearing winds. They are known as steppe in Asia, as pampas in Argentina, and as prairie in North America. In these areas rainfall totals are low, and most of the rain is in early summer during thunderstorms. Summers are hot and dry, but in winter the plains are swept by freezing winds and blizzards.

Until the 19th century these grasslands were home to vast herds of grazing animals such as the buffalo. Then the settlers moved in, converting the grasslands to cattle ranching and wheat growing areas. As a result, large areas of the North American prairies have become the world's 'bread basket'.

THE GREAT PLAINS

The Great Plains of the United States lie between the Rocky Mountains and the Mississippi Basin. In the 19th century white settlers drove the native Indians from the plains and used the grasses for cattle ranching. They were followed by wheat farmers, who ploughed up the uncultivated soils of the plains over a number of years that were wetter than average.

By the 1930s the series of wet years had given way to a series of dry years. The thin prairie soils, exposed to the dry winds with no grass to protect them, soon turned to dust and were blown away. Fields were changed into deserts, and thousands of homesteads had to be abandoned. The Dust Bowl, as it was known, ruined an entire generation of farmers, many of whom had to migrate to other parts of the United States.

Below: *The wetter parts of the North American prairies are some of the world's main grain-growing areas. The grasslands of the drier parts are used for cattle ranching.*

Wetlands

Wetlands include several kinds of environment: the mangrove swamps of coastal tropical areas; deltas and estuaries; salt marshes and lagoons; inland marshes, swamps, fens and ponds. Although the total area they occupy is relatively small, they are also vulnerable to misuse and damage by human populations.

Mangrove swamps

Mangroves are the tidal wetlands of tropical areas. Their vegetation includes sea grasses (flowering plants which bloom beneath the sea) and forest. They fringe more than half of all tropical coastlines, and have huge resources of fish and shellfish, particularly prawns and oysters, which local peoples depend on heavily. Mangroves absorb the impact of powerful tropical storms, preventing the erosion of low-lying, vulnerable coastlines, and protecting coastal towns from storm damage.

Salt marshes and estuaries

Salt marshes form tidal wetlands in temperate areas, and are found all round the coastlines of North America, north-western Europe, south-east Australia, and temperate South America. They are very important as a refuge for wildfowl, particularly for migrant birds during the colder months of winter.

Worldwide, estuaries cover twice the area of mangroves and salt marshes. They form

The wetlands of Chesapeake Bay are under constant threat from industries and the activities of surrounding cities.

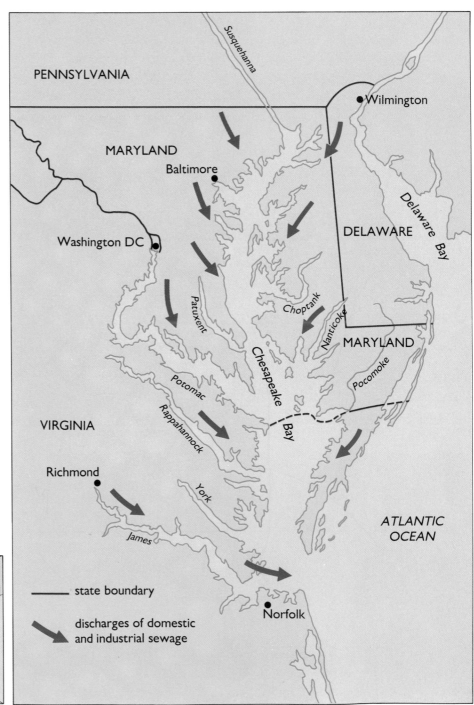

PENNSYLVANIA

Susquehanna

Wilmington

MARYLAND

Baltimore

Washington DC

DELAWARE

Delaware Bay

Patuxent

Choptank

Nanticoke

MARYLAND

Potomac

Chesapeake Bay

Pocomoke

Rappahannock

VIRGINIA

Richmond

York

ATLANTIC OCEAN

James

—— state boundary

discharges of domestic and industrial sewage

Norfolk

Chesapeake Bay

Baltimore

Washington

Chesapeake Bay

MISSISSIPPI DELTA

Norfolk

'tidal ponds', where sea-water and freshwater ecosystems meet, and are the most productive of coastal systems. Estuaries are thought to generate almost 80 million tonnes of fish a year, more than our entire annual catch from the sea. They also provide nurseries for young ocean-going fish. Along the eastern United States, up to 75 per cent of fished species spend some of their life cycles in estuaries.

Many people living on tropical coastlands depend on the mangrove swamps for fish. Inset below: Mangrove roots.

Wetlands under threat

Wetlands are some of the world's most threatened ecosystems, as almost two-thirds of the human population live close to them. Some major conurbations, such as Los Angeles and Tokyo, have almost destroyed their neighbouring wetland areas.

The major threats to wetlands include mangrove deforestation in South-east Asia, for woodchips; clearance and drainage of mangroves for farming; housing and industrial developments in densely populated areas; pollution from rubbish dumping, industrial wastes, and oil spillages; and poisoning of the waters, caused by concentration of fertilizers washed out from surrounding agricultural land.

WETLANDS OF THE USA

The southern and eastern coasts of the United States are rich in wetlands. The estuary of Chesapeake Bay on the Atlantic coast is one of the world's most productive ecosystems. But it is surrounded by several major cities such as Washington, Baltimore and Norfolk, which use the estuary for the disposal of industrial waste and sewage; as oil refinery and power station sites; and for recreation. Consequently the ecological richness of the bay is today in decline from human pollution.

On the Gulf of Mexico coast the Mississippi delta accounts for 40 per cent of the country's wetlands. A vast network of canals, built to exploit the delta's oil resources, has disrupted the area's natural fisheries. Dredged sludge is piled up to form banks, or levees, along the channels, interrupting the normal ebb and flow of the tides and currents into the marshlands.

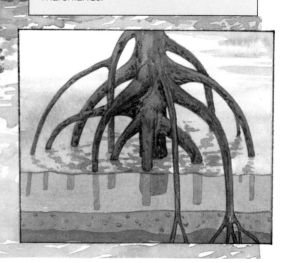

Desert Margins

The margins of deserts are very vulnerable to climatic variations. Here rainfall is usually just enough to promote a growth of poor grass and scrub, but some years there is no rain at all. Then, the nomadic peoples who inhabit desert margins have to migrate long distances with their herds and flocks to find pastures for grazing. Prolonged droughts over several years bring famine and severe hardship.

Desertification

During the last half century the deserts have begun to spread. Areas which were once able to support nomadic grazing and cultivation can now no longer do so. Desertification, as it is called, is partly a result of climatic change, with many desert margins having had a drier than average climate over many years.

Desertification has also been caused by increasing pressure on the land as populations have grown. The size of herds has increased, and more people are trying to grow food in the limited areas of cultivation around water-holes and oases. As a result, lands have become overgrazed, overcultivated, or stripped of trees for firewood. Plant life is reduced and the soil is easily eroded by the dry winds and torrential summer rains. Areas which once supported short savanna grass are turning into deserts.

Deserts are spreading on all continents, and each year some 12 million hectares (30 million acres) become agriculturally worthless. Some of the worst-affected areas are around the margins of the Sahara, but all desert margins are at risk. Even parts of southern Europe, such as the drier areas of Spain, are showing some of the signs of desertification by the worsening quality of pastures. It is likely that global warming will extend the desert margins still further.

Below: The areas at risk from desertification are in all continents. They include valuable grain growing lands in North America.

desert

risk of desertification

Scenes like these became commonplace in the Sahel countries in the 1980s. Massive relief efforts may not be enough to prevent future starvation on a huge scale.

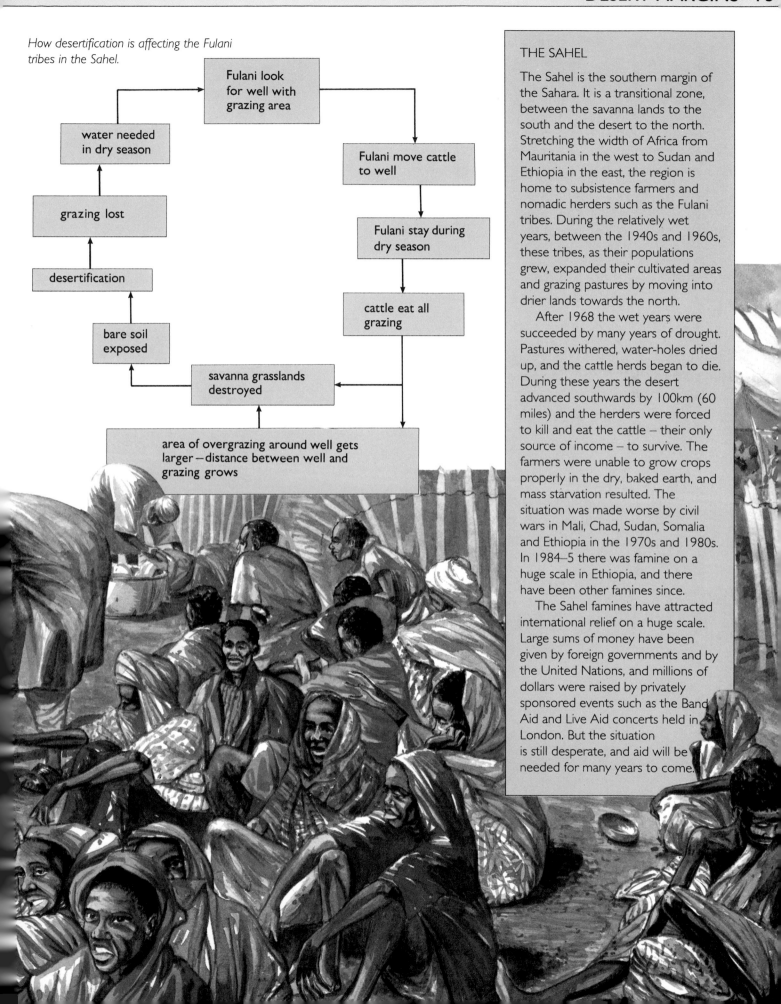

How desertification is affecting the Fulani tribes in the Sahel.

Fulani look for well with grazing area

water needed in dry season

Fulani move cattle to well

grazing lost

desertification

Fulani stay during dry season

bare soil exposed

cattle eat all grazing

savanna grasslands destroyed

area of overgrazing around well gets larger – distance between well and grazing grows

THE SAHEL

The Sahel is the southern margin of the Sahara. It is a transitional zone, between the savanna lands to the south and the desert to the north. Stretching the width of Africa from Mauritania in the west to Sudan and Ethiopia in the east, the region is home to subsistence farmers and nomadic herders such as the Fulani tribes. During the relatively wet years, between the 1940s and 1960s, these tribes, as their populations grew, expanded their cultivated areas and grazing pastures by moving into drier lands towards the north.

After 1968 the wet years were succeeded by many years of drought. Pastures withered, water-holes dried up, and the cattle herds began to die. During these years the desert advanced southwards by 100km (60 miles) and the herders were forced to kill and eat the cattle – their only source of income – to survive. The farmers were unable to grow crops properly in the dry, baked earth, and mass starvation resulted. The situation was made worse by civil wars in Mali, Chad, Sudan, Somalia and Ethiopia in the 1970s and 1980s. In 1984–5 there was famine on a huge scale in Ethiopia, and there have been other famines since.

The Sahel famines have attracted international relief on a huge scale. Large sums of money have been given by foreign governments and by the United Nations, and millions of dollars were raised by privately sponsored events such as the Band Aid and Live Aid concerts held in London. But the situation is still desperate, and aid will be needed for many years to come.

Frozen Wastes

The cold lands of the Earth are those whose average temperature in the hottest month is less than 10°C. Some of these lands are permanently covered by ice; others are not covered by ice but the ground remains frozen for most of the year. Until now, these areas have proved to be too cold and remote for exploitation of their resources on a large scale.

Polar zones

The two polar zones are very different from one another. The Arctic is virtually a land-locked ocean fringed by the northern continents. The surfaces crossed by Arctic explorers and scientific expeditions are not land, but massive floating rafts of ice. In the short northern summer the edges of this frozen sea melt and the pack ice turns to 'drift' ice. Great masses break away and drift southwards as icebergs. North of the Arctic Circle there are times in winter when the Sun never even rises, and times in the summer when it never sets.

By contrast, the Antarctic is a continental land mass covered with a cap of ice up to 2,300m (7,000ft) thick. In winter the ice spreads out over the surrounding ocean as ice shelves, with spectacular cliffs up to 60m (200ft) high. Like the Arctic, there are weeks of continuous night and continuous daylight, but at the opposite times of the year.

Tundras

South of the Arctic pack ice is a zone in which winter lasts for 9 or 10 months. During the short summer the surface layers of the ground thaw, but the lower layers remain frozen hard. They are called permafrost (from 'permanent frost').

CHANGE IN ALASKA

The traditional hunting and fishing life of the Alaskan Eskimo, or Inuit, has been changing in recent decades. The majority of Inuit now live not in tents or igloos but in permanent settlements and have regular jobs.

Much of the change has been brought about by the exploitation of Alaska's oil resources. The Trans-Alaska pipeline now carries oil south from the oilfields at Prudhoe Bay to the terminal at Valdez on the Pacific coast. Although oil has introduced new wealth to Alaska, it threatens to change forever the character of one of the world's few remaining wilderness areas.

The tundra landscape is a boggy, treeless area. Plant growth is possible in the brief summers, which are only a few weeks long.

The Arctic and Antarctic regions.

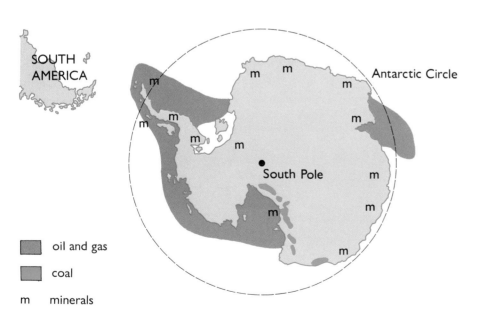

The growing season is too short and the winds too severe for trees to survive, but there is a brief flowering of lichens and quick-growing plants. Because the ground is frozen at depth, water cannot easily drain away, and much of the surface is boggy.

Animals and people have adapted to the severe conditions. Herds of caribou survive by migrating long distances each summer to new grazing grounds, where they feed on lichen by scraping away the overlying snow. Another native animal, the musk-ox, has a very thick coat to protect it from the winter. Some two million people live in the cold tundra regions of Alaska, northern Canada, northern Scandinavia and Russia, but the traditional Arctic ways of life based on hunting and fishing are now changing.

Frozen resources
The cold areas of the world are rich in untapped resources. The Arctic contains some of the Earth's richest fisheries in the shallow waters on the surrounding continental shelf. Both the Arctic and Antarctic regions have enormous reserves of oil, gas and other minerals. Antarctica does not belong to any one country but is managed by the 16 states which signed the Antarctic Treaty, seven of whom have territorial rights in the continent. The future of Antarctica and of its huge resources has yet to be fully worked out.

Mountains

All continents contain mountain ranges that rise to more than 2,500m (8,200ft). Since climate and vegetation change as altitude increases, mountain ranges provide a variety of environments. People who live and farm in the mountains have to come to terms with this.

Altitude, climate and vegetation

On the lower slopes of mountains where temperatures are higher and the land is sheltered, there is usually denser forest. With increases in height the temperature falls, and beyond a certain level, known as the tree line, it is too cold for forest to grow. Grasses become the main vegetation, until a level is reached where only so-called Arctic or alpine plants can grow. Higher still, above the 'snow line', there is permanent ice and snow. The height of the snow line depends on the direction in which the mountain slope faces. On north-facing slopes snow lies much longer and at a lower level than on south-facing ones, which receive much more sunshine.

Mountains and people

Mountains are inhospitable environments for people. There are few places where they can settle and transport is slow and difficult. The steep slopes, heavy rain and strong winds create problems for agriculture and increase the likelihood of soil erosion. Also, the low atmospheric pressure and reduced oxygen content of the air make breathing more difficult, while the thinner air exposes the skin to more of the Sun's harmful radiation. Visitors to the mountains find these conditions a problem,

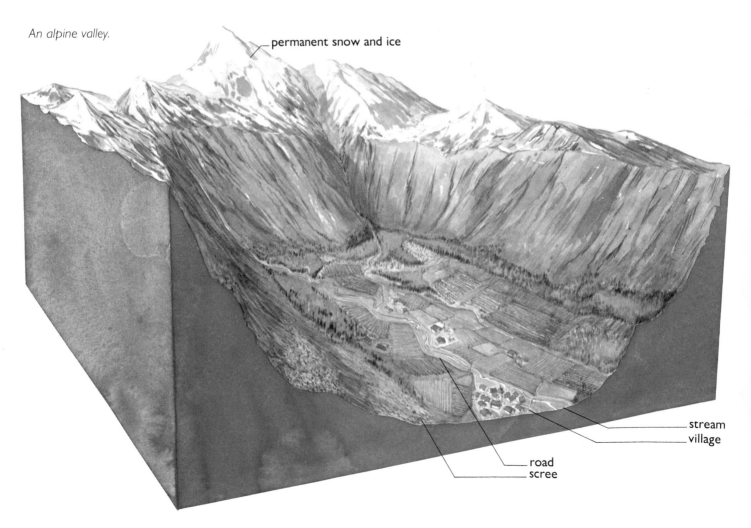

An alpine valley.

permanent snow and ice

stream
village
road
scree

but local people have, over time, adapted to them.

In tropical areas mountains can bring some benefits. The rain forest zones of the lower slopes give way to a more pleasant, cooler type of climate further up. Here temperate food crops such as wheat or potatoes can be grown. In East Africa the plateau lands of Zimbabwe, Zambia, Uganda and neighbouring countries were attractive to European colonists in the 19th century because of their comfortable climates.

Some mountain people have adapted to their environment by transhumance, the name given to the seasonal movement of livestock. Herdsmen and their families migrate up the mountain slopes in spring so that animals can graze the high pastures in summer. The community then returns to the valley bottoms in autumn, often carrying down hay as a winter fodder crop.

Machu Picchu, the lost Inca city, occupied a hilltop site high in the Andes.

THE PERUVIAN ANDES

High in the Andes of Peru is Machu Picchu, a sacred city of the ancient Inca civilization. Machu Picchu, which appears to have been used for the worship of the Incan sun god, was only rediscovered by chance in 1913. From their capital at Cuzco the Incas ruled a huge empire which stretched the length of the northern Andes, until it was destroyed by the Spanish invaders in the 16th century.

Today the Peruvian Indians lead a hard life as village farmers. They grow potatoes and vegetables, graze cattle and llamas on the mountain slopes, and trade in local markets. Some Indians find work in silver and zinc mines.

Travel in the Andes is still slow. One traveller's journey from Lima to Cuzco, about 500km (310 miles), began with a railway journey to Huancayo. This included an eight-hour climb of 4,800m (15,800ft) by way of many tunnels, bridges and zigzag bends. Of the journey he wrote: *The air became thinner. A doctor walked along the corridor carrying an oxygen tube. Suddenly everything turned black. I leant back in my seat, and cold sweat broke out on my forehead. I was terribly sick; my limbs ached as if I'd got 'flu.*

The remainder of the journey, which took eight days in all, was over rough mountain roads in a crowded bus and truck.

New Land

In some parts of the world new environments have been created by reclamation of land from the sea. Indeed, in places where people are running out of living space, land reclamation can offer a way of satisfying the needs for new housing, industries and agriculture, and even new cities.

The Netherlands

The Netherlands has more reclaimed land than any other country. Land reclamation has been taking place there for many centuries, and today 40 per cent of the country lies below sea-level and is reclaimed land. Reclamation is carried out by building dikes (raised embankments) to enclose the area to be reclaimed, and then pumping out the sea-water to expose the land beneath. The reclaimed areas, called polders, include the land where farming is most intensive, but the ground has to be kept dry by continuous pumping. In earlier centuries this was done by windmills, which became a distinctive feature of the Dutch landscape.

In the present century, modern machinery and engineering have enabled reclamation in the Netherlands to be carried out on a large scale. The great sea inlet to northern Holland, called the Zuider Zee, has been steadily reclaimed by creating four large polders covering an area of 145,000 hectares (350,000 acres). The water remaining has been turned into a freshwater lake, the Ijssel Meer, by building a 30-km (19-mile) barrier dam across the outlet to the sea. Reclamation of the last remaining polder, the Markerwaard, is still going on.

The Zuider Zee scheme has enabled the Dutch not only to create more agricultural land for food, but also to find sites for new towns. The planners are using the polders as 'overspill' areas for surplus population from the overcrowded Amsterdam region. On the East Flevoland polder, the new town of Lelystad supplies the everyday needs of the surrounding region.

Land for ports

The Dutch have also reclaimed land for harbour expansion and industrial development. Rotterdam, the world's biggest port, has steadily grown

'God made the land but the Dutch made Holland.' This saying emphasizes how much of their own country the Dutch have created for themselves by reclaiming land from the sea.

Map

Legend:
- land below sea-level
- dry interior regions
- gas fields
- coal field
- • cities

Groningen

Ijssel Meer reclamation scheme

Wieringermeer

ZUIDER ZEE

Lelystad

N.E. Polder

Markerwaard

East Flevoland

Haarlem

South Flevoland

Amsterdam

NORTH SEA

Enschede

Leiden

The Hague

Utrecht

Lek

Arnhem

Europoort

Rotterdam

Maasvlakte

Waal

delta scheme

Eindhoven

Maas

Rhine

Schelde

Maastricht

westwards towards the open sea, as ships have become larger and deeper harbours are needed. To this end, the outports of Europoort (opened in 1960) and Maasvlakte (opened in 1974) were built for large bulk carriers and oil tankers. They were constructed on reclaimed land, and are now sites of vast industrial complexes.

Above: A typical polder landscape. Farms and roads are laid out in a regular pattern on the newly reclaimed land.

Below: The outports of Europoort and Maasvlakte in Rotterdam.

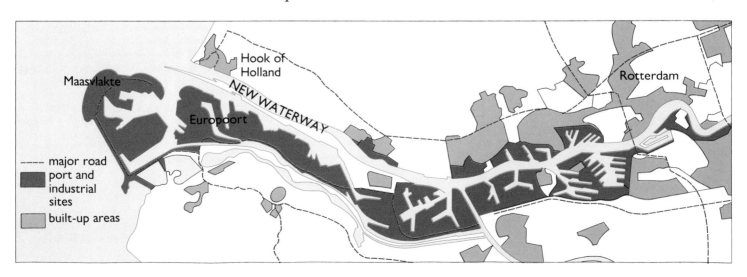

Maasvlakte
Hook of Holland
NEW WATERWAY
Europoort
Rotterdam

----- major road
■ port and industrial sites
▨ built-up areas

Pollution

Pollution is the harming of the environment by largely manufactured substances. Air, water and land are all at risk from pollutants. Excessive noise is now also considered as a form of pollution. Throughout the world, pollution is being recognized as a major environmental problem.

Atmospheric pollution

Some pollutants in the atmosphere occur naturally – for instance, volcanic eruptions and vegetation decay add to the amount of carbon dioxide in the atmosphere. But the growth of industrial societies has greatly increased the quantity of air pollutants, including carbon dioxide, carbon monoxide, lead and sulphur.

Some of the principal ways in which the environment can become polluted.

Each year, 500,000 tonnes of lead is released into the air, much of it from vehicle exhausts. Lead is added to petrol to make it burn more efficiently. However, once in the atmosphere it is breathed into the human body and may cause blood disorders, especially in children. In Western countries the introduction of unleaded petrol is helping to ease the problem, but in much of the Third World levels of lead in petrol are dangerously high.

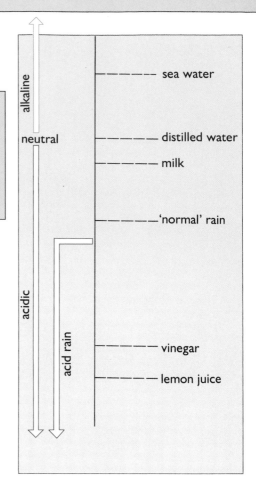

Above: *This diagram shows how acid rain compares for acidity with some well known drinks and other fluids.*

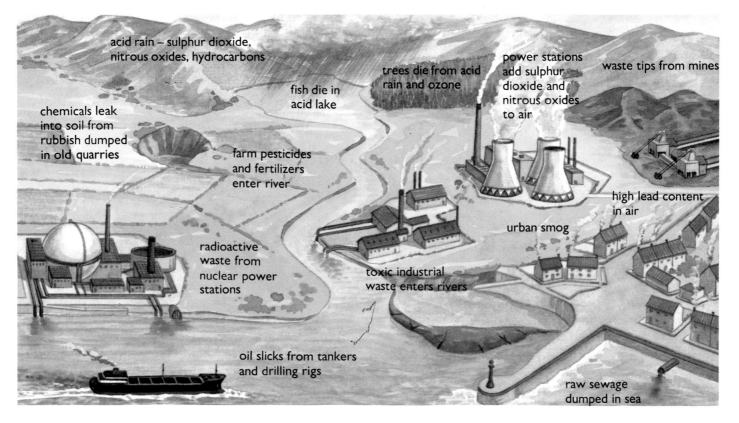

The problem of lead pollution is worst in the cities of the Third World. City centres crammed with vehicles using high-leaded petrol emit harmful fumes into the air all day long.

Acid rain

The presence of sulphur dioxides and nitrogen oxides in the atmosphere is due mainly to coal-fired power stations and other industrial plants. Once airborne, these gases change into dilute solutions of sulphuric and nitric acids, which later fall as rain – known as acid rain – often far from where they were first produced. For example, power stations in Britain are responsible for acid gases that are blown by the wind over Norway and Sweden.

Acid rain destroys wide areas of forest, and also runs into rivers and lakes, where it becomes increasingly concentrated, and eventually kills off fish and other aquatic life. As a result, some Scandinavian lakes have become 'dead'.

Other countries are also suffering badly from acid rain, including Germany and its forests. Some of the worst-hit countries are Czechoslovakia and Hungary, where until recently there had been little control of atmospheric pollution by industry.

To reduce the acidity of emissions from power stations some countries are now introducing desulphurization plants, but it will be years before this has a noticeable effect on acid rain.

Land and water pollution

Land pollution is due mainly to the disposal of liquid and solid wastes. In the past a lot of rubbish was biodegradable, meaning that it would decay naturally, but today many wastes are of non-degradable substances such as plastics. A lot of this waste is dumped in landfill sites, such as old quarries or mines, or simply piled up in rubbish tips which may become a major health hazard. To help solve the problem, biodegradable substances are now being reintroduced.

Many inland and coastal waters have also been polluted. Much of the pollution is due to the careless disposal of industrial wastes and sewage. Over half the rivers in the United States have been officially declared unfit for drinking or for recreation. Further pollution of coastlines comes from oil slicks caused by spillages from tankers. Even after a massive clean-up operation, it may be years before the beaches are clean enough to support wildlife once again or be used for bathing.

Resources and Conservation

Until recently, most people regarded the environment as there to be exploited for economic gain. Today we realize that over-exploitation of the environment is ruining it for future generations. Many people now appreciate the need to conserve it and to use its resources less wastefully.

The disposal of household waste. We need to find ways of recycling more of it.

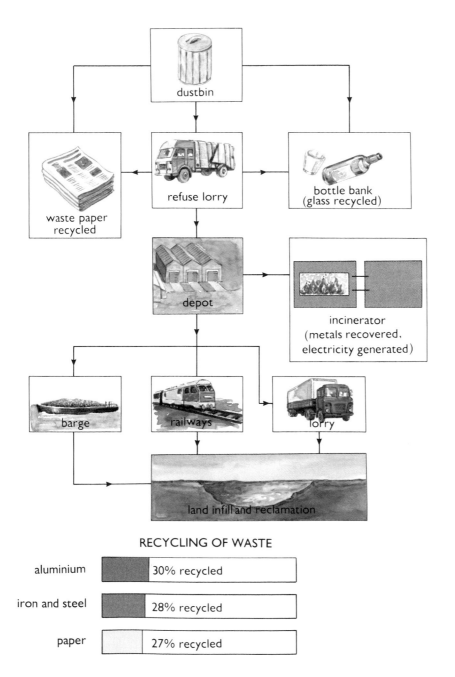

dustbin

waste paper recycled

refuse lorry

bottle bank (glass recycled)

depot

incinerator (metals recovered, electricity generated)

barge

railways

lorry

land infill and reclamation

RECYCLING OF WASTE

aluminium	30% recycled
iron and steel	28% recycled
paper	27% recycled

A throw-away society

Because of the waste it produces, Western society has been called a 'throw-away' society. The United States, the world's most industrialized country, creates more than 400 million tonnes of industrial waste and 200 million tonnes of household waste every year. This includes 7 million cars, 20 million tonnes of waste paper, 48 billion tin cans and 26 billion bottles. Other industrialized countries also produce large amounts of waste. Even finding some way or somewhere to dispose of all this is a major problem.

In today's society the continuous consumption of goods has become an end in itself. Advertising and the media are encouraging us all the time to acquire and use more products. Technical developments, such as the use of new materials, together with rapidly changing fashions, mean that things soon become out-of-date and are discarded. This approach to living, until recently confined to Western countries, is already seen in wealthier places in the Third World, and in eastern Europe.

However, at last people are beginning to recognize that the resources needed to continue this spiral of economic growth are finite, and that the future may lie in conservation rather than consumption. One approach is to make better use of resources by recycling, or reusing scrap materials. Iron, aluminium and paper are readily recycled, and so old cars, drinks cans and newspapers need no longer be wasted. Major businesses are also emerging to recycle waste chemicals and oil.

Conserving the environment

Conservation is about protecting and preserving the environment. Damage can be caused by pollution, industrial developments, or even overuse by people for leisure. Areas sensitive to environmental damage include countryside, mountains, forests, wetlands

Nepal is trying to develop a strategy which integrates conservation with development.

and coasts. In Britain certain measures have been taken to protect these areas from overuse. They include creating National Parks in the most scenic areas; designating other scenic areas as 'Areas of Outstanding Natural Beauty', and 1,000km (620 miles) of coastline as 'Heritage Coast'; giving legal protection to important natural, scientific and archaeological sites; and paying farmers not to cultivate sensitive environments.

Environmental conservation is not confined to industrial countries such as Britain. Many Third World countries have also taken steps to protect their environments.

CONSERVATION IN NEPAL

Nepal is a mountainous, forested country in the Himalayas. It depends heavily on its timber for fuel, but also has some of the world's least-exploited forests, with many rare breeds of animals. Nepal has set up a national conservation strategy, which includes the creation of a National Park to protect rare animals such as the endangered rhino and tiger; the building of hydroelectric dams, carefully sited to protect valley farmlands; and a reforestation programme to supply fuelwood, prevent soil erosion and control the release of water into major rivers. Another part of the strategy is, more simply, to develop new pneumatic tyres to increase the carrying capacity of traditional bullock carts.

References

Acid rain The pollution of rainfall from nitrogen and sulphur dioxides in the atmosphere.

Biome A community of plants and animals which extends over a large natural area. Most biomes are types of forest or grassland.

Boreal forest The coniferous forests of cold temperate areas, also called 'taiga'.

Conservation The protection and preservation of the environment from overuse or damage.

Consumer society A society which sustains its economy through the continual production and consumption of goods.

Desertification The extension of the margins of deserts. Long periods of drought, as well as overpopulation, over-grazing and over-cultivation all contribute to desertification. Soil erosion, crop failure and starvation for local peoples are often the result.

Dust Bowl The devastation of much of the Great Plains of the United States by wind erosion during the 1930s, when many wheat-growing lands had to be abandoned.

Ecosystem A natural system in which plants, animals, soils and people are linked by flows of energy and nutrients. Heat from the Sun is the main energy source.

Flow The movement of energy or material through a natural system, for example, water flowing in a stream, or nutrients being absorbed from the soil by plants.

Food chain The different levels in an ecosystem whereby one level provides the food needs of the next higher level; for example, carnivores (flesh eaters) prey on herbivores (grazing animals).

Humus The organic constituent of soil. Humus results from the decay of plants, trees, animals and other organic wastes.

Hydrological cycle The circulation of water in its various forms through the atmosphere, soil, plants, rivers, and the oceans.

Infiltration The percolation of rainwater through the layers of the soil.

Leaching The washing out from soil of soluble minerals (bases) by percolating rainwater. Leaching makes a soil more acidic and less fertile.

Loam A soil with a balanced texture, a mixture of sand, silt and clay particles. Loamy soils provide good farming land.

Mangrove Forest and shrub areas which grow along low-lying tropical coastlines. The vegetation grows directly from the sea-bed.

Nomadism A way of life that involves moving from place to place in search of water and pastures for grazing herds. It is the traditional way of life in semi-arid savanna or steppe regions.

Pampas The steppe or temperate grassland areas of Argentina and Uruguay.

Permafrost The frozen ground of tundra regions. During the summer the upper layer may thaw for a short time (the active layer) but the ground at depth remains permanently frozen.

Polder An area of land reclaimed from the sea in the Netherlands.

Prairie The temperate grasslands of the United States and Canada. The wetter parts of the prairies are wheat-growing areas; the drier parts are used for cattle ranching.

Recycling Converting waste, such as metals, paper and glass into reusable materials.

Salt marsh The marsh lands of coastal areas. Salt marshes provide habitats for many bird and wildlife species of coastal areas. *See* **Wetland.**

Savanna Tropical grassland, developed under 'wet and dry' season conditions. True savanna is a mixture of grassland and trees. Towards the rain forest margins the trees become denser; towards the desert margin the grass is mixed with scrub.

Selva *See* **Tropical rain forest.**

Snow line The lowest level of continuous snow cover on a mountain slope. The snow line varies seasonally and also according to the slope's aspect (the direction it is facing).

Soil erosion The wearing away of the soil by wind and rain. Continuous soil erosion can make the land infertile.

Steppe Temperate grassland. *See* **Prairie.**

Store A point within a natural system where material remains for a time, for example, water within a lake, or in the sea.

Transhumance The seasonal migration of farmers with their herds and flocks from valley bottoms to higher mountain pastures.

Transpiration The emission of water from plant tissues on to the plant surface, followed by its evaporation. The total loss of water is called evapotranspiration.

Tree line The highest level of continuous tree cover on a mountain slope.

Tropical rain forest The natural vegetation of hot, wet, tropical areas. The tall trees provide a dense canopy which shades out smaller trees. In many areas of the tropics forests are being cleared for timber, new settlements and agriculture.

Tundra The environment and vegetation of cold areas around and close to the Arctic Circle. Tundras are open, windswept regions with low-growing shrubs and plants, no trees, and boggy tracts caused by poor drainage.

Vegetation succession The sequence of change which leads to bare surfaces eventually becoming covered by trees or other tall-growing types of vegetation.

Wetland An area of marshes, swamps or fens. Many wetlands are coastal tidal areas, deltas or estuaries.

Population

The World's Peoples

How people are spread out over the Earth's surface is called population distribution. If the world's population were distributed evenly over the land area each of us would have a piece of ground measuring 0.028 square kilometres (0.0108 square miles). In fact, population is distributed very unevenly.

The population spread

Along with China and India, the most densely populated parts of the world are Japan, Europe and eastern parts of North America. These last three are also industrialized regions where most people live in towns or cities. Urbanization, or the adoption of an urban way of life, is spreading quickly to many countries of the southern hemisphere, particularly in South America.

Many other parts of the world have few people, because the climate or terrain is unsuitable. For instance, desert regions such as the Sahara, Arabian peninsula, central Asia, and parts of western Australia, are too dry to grow crops, and so population is limited to nomadic groups or mining settlements. Other areas are

World population density. Even with the rapid population increase of modern times, many areas of the world are likely to remain uninhabited.

THE WORLD'S MOST DENSELY POPULATED COUNTRIES		
		persons per km^2
1	Monaco	18,121
2	Macau	17,150
3	Hong Kong	5,364
4	Gibraltar	4,472
5	Singapore	4,215
6	Malta	1,267
7	Bermuda	1,120
8	Bangladesh	722
9	Bahrain	667
10	Barbados	630
11	Mauritius	532
12	Taiwan	519
13	Netherlands	424
14	South Korea	414
15	Puerto Rico	382
16	Grenada	373
17	San Marino	367
18	Saint Vincent	347
19	Belgium	329
20	Japan	323
21	Martinique	297
22	Lebanon	264
23	El Salvador	257
24	India	251
25	Sri Lanka	240
26	Rwanda	236
27	United Kingdom	230

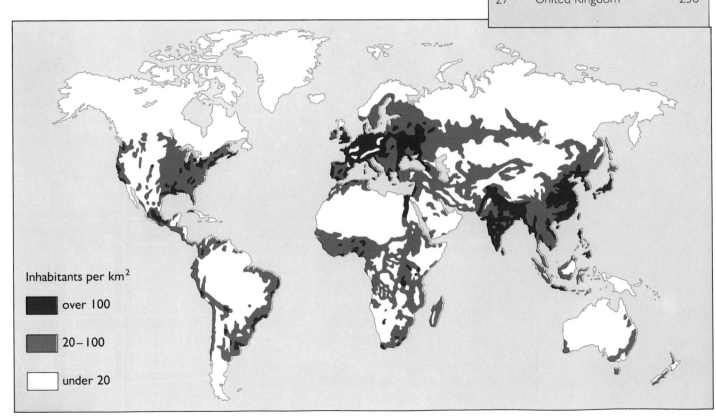

Inhabitants per km^2

- over 100
- 20–100
- under 20

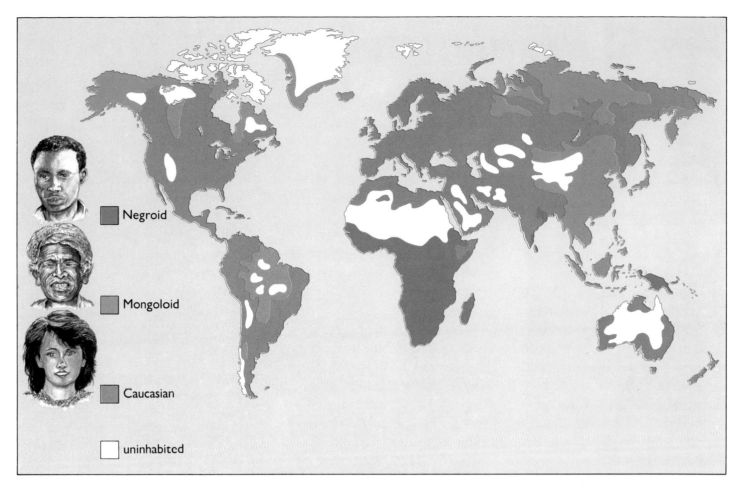

The major racial groups. Many people find themselves living far from their original homelands.

- Negroid
- Mongoloid
- Caucasian
- uninhabited

too cold to grow crops or attract large settlements, and are very remote from more populated places. They include the tundra areas of Siberia, and the ice-caps of Greenland and Antarctica.

Until a few decades ago the tropical rain forests of Central Africa, South America and the East Indies were very sparsely populated because they were difficult to penetrate and clear. However, some tropical forests, such as those in Brazil, are now attracting more settlers. Mountain areas such as the Andes and Himalayas are also not popular places to live. Transport is difficult,

SOME POPULATION FACTS

Less than 10 per cent of people live in the southern hemisphere.
Only about 0.3 per cent of people live north of 60°N.
China alone has a quarter of the world's population, while China, together with India, Russia and the United States contain over half of the world's people.
Some of the most densely populated countries such as Monaco, Hong Kong and Singapore are also the smallest.

while thin soils and low temperatures mean that few crops grow well. Initially people find it difficult to breathe and live at high altitudes, though eventually they adapt and acclimatize to the conditions.

The world's races

Although there are many races in the world, with different cultures, religions and languages, most of the world's people come from three basic ethnic groups: Caucasian, Mongoloid and Negroid. Over the centuries many races were dispersed far from their homelands.

In particular, Europeans, through colonization in the 18th and 19th centuries, spread and left their culture all over the world. The slave trade in the 18th century established large Negroid minorities in North and South America. War and political conflicts in the last century have created movements of refugees, especially in Africa and South-east Asia.

World Population Growth

There are twice as many people in the world today as there were 50 years ago. By the year 2000 the world's population is likely to exceed six billion, and by 2100 may have reached 10 billion. The population explosion – the rapid rate of population growth – is one of the most serious problems that the world faces.

Which areas are growing?
Population growth is not taking place evenly throughout the world. Until 50 years ago most of the growth was in Europe and the industrialized countries of the world. Now the populations of these countries are largely stable. Growth in recent decades has been mostly in the developing countries of South America, Africa and Asia. Some of the cities in these countries are already among the largest in the world.

There are several reasons for this growth. The standard of living has been improving for some people, despite the very poor living conditions of millions of others. Moreover, diseases such as cholera and smallpox can now be kept under control, and safer water supplies help to reduce the spread of disease. All these are factors that contribute to a reduction in the death rate. But because people often have little security in jobs or homes, they prefer to have large families on whom they can depend. Even though many children still die at birth or in infancy, the combination of falling death rates and high birth rates keeps population increases high.

World population growth. The populations of the developing countries of Asia, Africa and South America are growing far more quickly than those of Europe and North America, where populations are now largely stable.

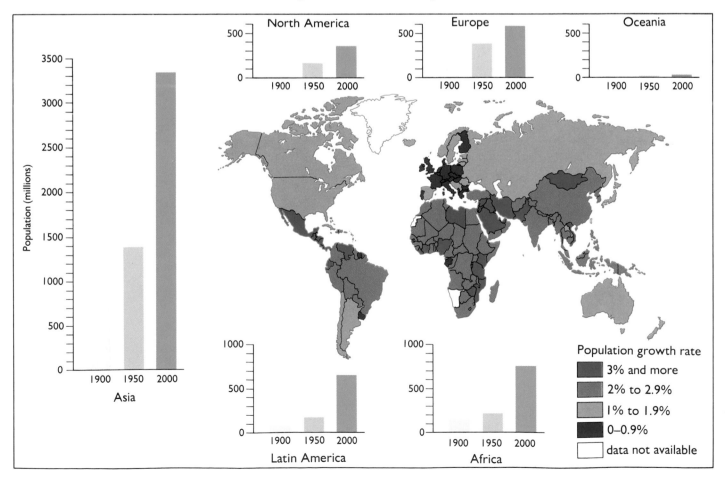

Right: The world population problem cannot be solved until birth rates come down to the level of death rates. The problem is most severe in the developing continents.

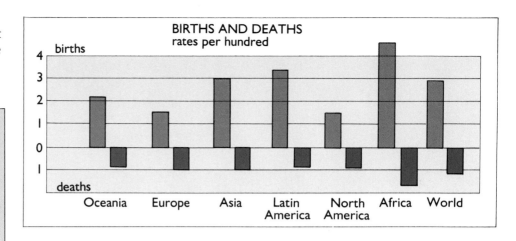

PYRAMIDS OF PEOPLE

Populations can be shown as pyramids, in which each age group is represented by a bar. The length of the bar shows the proportion of people in that age group. The pyramid for India has a broad base and a narrow top. This means that its population has a large number of young people, and is likely to grow considerably in the years ahead as many of these become parents. The small number of over-65s indicates that few people survive long enough to reach old age.

By contrast the pyramids for Canada and France are narrower at the base and broader higher up – indicating that families are smaller and people live longer. The world's population as a whole will get 'older' during the next century.

Problems of the next century

Continued population growth will mean a shortage of jobs, particularly for young people, and developed countries will have to find new land for housing. In the rural areas of developing countries there will be too little land for people to grow food, and a shortage of food at prices that people can afford. Famines and mass hunger, like the famines in Ethiopia and the Sudan in the 1980s, will become more common. Also, doctors, clinics, schools, fuel and safe drinking water will increasingly be in short supply. Some people who live in cities will be better off, but most of the inhabitants will still be poor.

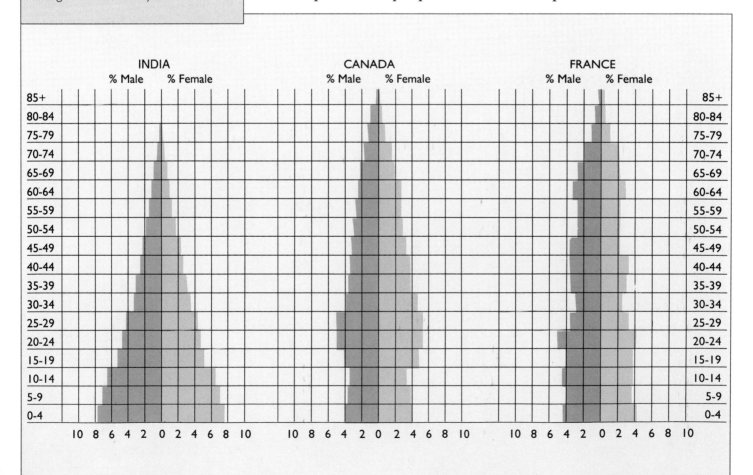

Nations of the World

There are over 180 nation states in the world today. The number of countries has grown rapidly since 1945 as former colonial territories have achieved independence and nationhood. More recently, the breakup of Yugoslavia and the former Soviet Union has added several more countries.

The United Nations

The United Nations (UN) was created in 1945 to promote world peace and cooperation between nations. Almost all nations now belong to it. Each member country has a seat and one vote in the General Assembly, which meets to discuss international problems

The United Nations has its headquarters in New York. Its main forum for discussion is the General Assembly, but its structure includes many other councils and agencies.

International Court of Justice

Economic & Social Council (looks after UN agencies)

Trusteeship Council (looks after Trust Terr.)

Security Council (tries to keep the peace between countries)

The Secretariat (civil servants who run the UN)

UN AGENCIES UNDP UNESCO

and disputes. Major international disputes are dealt with by the UN Security Council. This has 15 members, including the United States, Russia, China, France and Britain. The United Nations has several specialized agencies such as the UN Development Programme (UNDP) and Educational, Scientific and Cultural Organization (UNESCO).

During its lifetime the United Nations has intervened in several international disputes. One of the first was during the Korean War of 1950–3. Since then, UN peacekeeping forces have been to the island of Cyprus, to the Lebanon, to Iraq, and to Bosnia, which was once part of Yugoslavia.

TOWARDS A CLOSER WORLD?

Since the 1950s a number of organizations have been set up to promote closer economic cooperation between countries. They include:

European Community (EC)
The long-term aim of its twelve member nations is to bring about economic and political integration in Europe. It is one of the world's most powerful economic organizations. Many African, Caribbean and Pacific countries are linked to it.

Organization of Petroleum Exporting Countries (OPEC)
The main oil-producing countries, especially from the Middle East, belong to OPEC, which controls most of the world's oil supply and oil prices.

Organization of African Unity (OAU)
Its aim is to end colonial influences in African countries. It has 52 members.

Association of South-East Asian Nations (ASEAN)
Closer political and economic cooperation among the non-Communist states of the region is its main aim.

Organization of American States (OAS)
Its main concern is development aid from North American to South American countries.

The British Commonwealth
Although it has no formal aims, it maintains ties between 50 states that formerly belonged to the British Empire.

Commonwealth of Independent States (CIS)
The CIS maintains links between some of the countries of the former Soviet Union.

Some people think that the growth of organizations like these shows that the world as a whole is moving towards closer economic integration and interdependence. Others believe that international organizations can, at best, do little to help conflicts between nations.

Religions and Languages

Many people would say that they have a religion, though the numbers who practise their religion are fewer. As with some races of people, so religions have spread far from their places of origin. Religion and language are major factors in uniting people into a common culture.

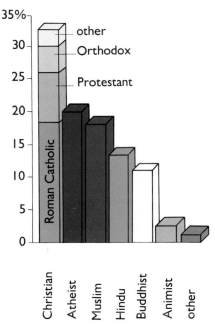

Above and below: *The main religions of the world have spread well beyond their homeland areas.*

The spread of religions

Christianity, Islam and Judaism are religions that all began in the Middle East. They are monotheistic religions, that is, they each have their own single god. Christianity spread to Europe from the 5th century during the period known as the Dark Ages. From the 15th century, Europeans who went to North and South America as conquerors or settlers took it there. Its most rapid growth in recent times has been in Africa. Islam has a huge following over much of northern Africa and in parts of eastern Asia. Judaism, the oldest of the three, is the religion of Israel, but is also found in Europe, Russia, and especially in the United States.

By contrast, Hinduism and Buddhism have remained largely the religions of India and eastern Asia respectively, where they are followed by hundreds of millions of people. There are also smaller followings of these religions in other parts of the world.

Below: *Many cities now have multi-ethnic populations. Newcomers from different cultures sometimes find it hard to adjust to new ways of life.*

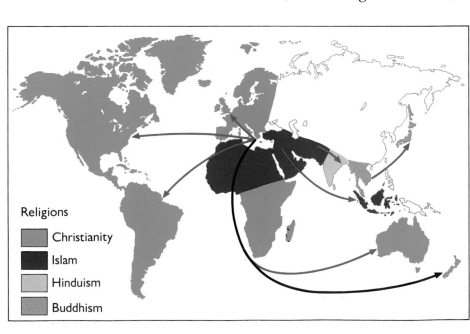

Religions
- Christianity
- Islam
- Hinduism
- Buddhism

In Russia and other countries which once belonged to the Soviet Union, politicians were for many years opposed to religion because they believed it harmed the state. They closed churches and other holy places and sometimes even imprisoned religious leaders. Today Russian people are much freer to follow their faith.

Many tongues

Today there are about 4,000 languages spoken in the world. These fall into 41 major groups, but each has many variations and dialects. On the continent of Africa alone there are well over 1,000 spoken languages. Some languages, like religions, have moved far from their home areas.

English, which is one of the many Germanic languages, is the principal language of many Commonwealth countries (those that once belonged to the British Empire). Even in African and Asian countries which have their own languages, English is often the language of business and written communication. In former French colonies in Africa and the West Indies, the people are bilingual – they speak two languages, their own language and French – or they speak just French. For similar historical reasons, the language of Quebec province in Canada is French, though most people in Canada are English-speaking. The main languages of South America are Spanish and Portuguese, which were introduced by colonizers from Spain and Portugal.

A century ago a universal language – one that everyone could speak – was invented. It was called Esperanto, but was never really successful. It seems unlikely that people will ever be able to share a common language.

English, French, Spanish and Portuguese – the world's main language groups – are the official languages of many countries.

A sense of belonging

Nationality, race, religion and language all contribute to a sense of identity. In other words, they help us to answer questions about who we are, where we come from and where we belong.

In today's world there are many people who find these questions difficult to answer. Migrants and refugees may find themselves living in unfamiliar surroundings among people who follow a different lifestyle. In one study of ethnic groups living in London, only a few people regarded themselves as 'English'. Others described themselves as Black English, West Indian, Jamaican, or even Londoners. London also contains many people of Asian, Indian, Pakistani and Chinese origin.

Modern communications like air travel, telephones and television make it easier for people to keep in touch with their origins, but also to live at a distance from them.

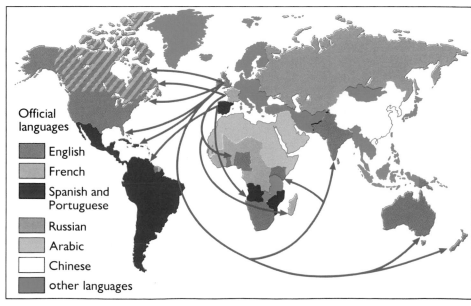

Official languages

- English
- French
- Spanish and Portuguese
- Russian
- Arabic
- Chinese
- other languages

Rich and Poor

The world's wealth is shared out unevenly. The richest countries, which hold about one-fifth of the world's population, receive two-thirds of the world's income, while the poorer countries, which contain three-quarters of the world's people, have only one-fifth of the total wealth. Moreover, the gap between the rich and the poor countries is widening.

A world map

The map of the world shown below features the world's thirty most populous countries. Some countries have relatively large populations in proportion to their land areas, for example Bangladesh, the United Kingdom and Japan. This means that they are densely populated. Other countries, such as Canada and Australia, do not appear on the map at all because their populations are small even though they have large land areas.

The world's richest countries include the United States and most countries of western Europe. These are commonly known as Western countries or are referred to collectively as the 'West'. Japan, Hong Kong and Singapore are Asian countries which are in the wealthiest category, and Japan is now considered as part of the 'West'. All these countries are said to be industrialized or developed.

China and India, besides being the most populated countries, are also among the poorest. Here, as in Pakistan and Bangladesh, large populations make it difficult to raise living standards since there are always so many people to be fed and housed. The poorer countries are said to be 'developing' or to belong to the 'developing world', or Third World. Many of the poorest are in Africa, and include those torn by famine and civil wars in recent years, such as Ethiopia and Sudan.

Some countries are not as wealthy as they appear to be. The 'oil-rich' states of the Middle East, such as Saudi Arabia, appear in the 'wealthy'

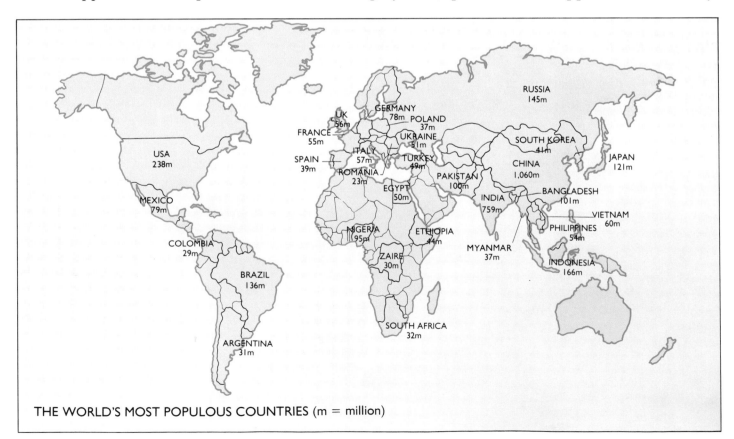

THE WORLD'S MOST POPULOUS COUNTRIES (m = million)

category, but generally the wealth is owned by the very small number of people who own and control the oil resources, and many people living there are still very poor.

North and South

The geography of rich and poor is sometimes seen in terms of North and South. Most of the better-off countries lie in the northern hemisphere, although Australia and New Zealand are exceptions. The wealth of these countries is

Right: *Many poorer countries of the South still depend on the sale of agricultural products (like the sugar cane shown here) or raw materials to the North.*

based on their range of manufactured goods and services, which they also sell to the poorer countries unable to provide them for themselves.

The poorer countries lie mostly in the southern part of the world. Although some of them have made progress with industrialization programmes, their economies are still based mainly on farm produce and raw materials such as minerals, which they sell to the northern industrialized countries. The money they receive, which is never enough for their needs, helps them to buy from the North the manufactured goods, services and technical know-how they require if they are to develop further.

Above: *The wealthy countries of the North sell their industrial products and commercial services (such as banking or insurance) to poorer countries.*

An unequal world

Over the last generation the richer countries have been growing richer still, and the poorer countries have lagged further and further behind. Many poor countries have tried to pay for economic development by borrowing vast sums of money from rich countries such as the United States. However, the money was always lent at interest, and this has now grown so great that some poor countries cannot afford to repay the interest on the loans.

War and Conflict

Although the last world war ended in 1945, since then there have been over 160 armed conflicts in the world, in which more than 16 million people – mostly civilians – have been killed. Every year, there are about a dozen or more wars going on in the world.

The superpowers and the Cold War

In Europe the development, after 1945, of the North Atlantic Treaty Organization (NATO), led by the United States, and the Warsaw Pact, led by the Soviet Union, caused a build-up of arms and international tension between the two 'superpower' blocs. This was the period known as the Cold War. Some people believe, however, that it was the military strength of both these alliances, and in particular their nuclear weapons, that prevented real war from breaking out between them.

Since the late 1980s the tension between the eastern Communist and western non-Communist 'free' countries has largely disappeared. Political revolutions in eastern Europe and the Soviet Union swept the old Communist governments from power, and Germany was reunited. The Cold War began to come to an end as both the USA and

WORLD ARMAMENTS

Since 1945 the quantities of arms in the world have increased enormously. The United States and Russia still have stockpiles of nuclear weapons large enough to destroy the world several times over. Many countries in the Third World have built up large armies at great expense. Iraq and Libya have used some of their oil revenues to buy expensive modern weapons. Vietnam and North Korea are poor countries, but they maintain some of the world's largest armies.

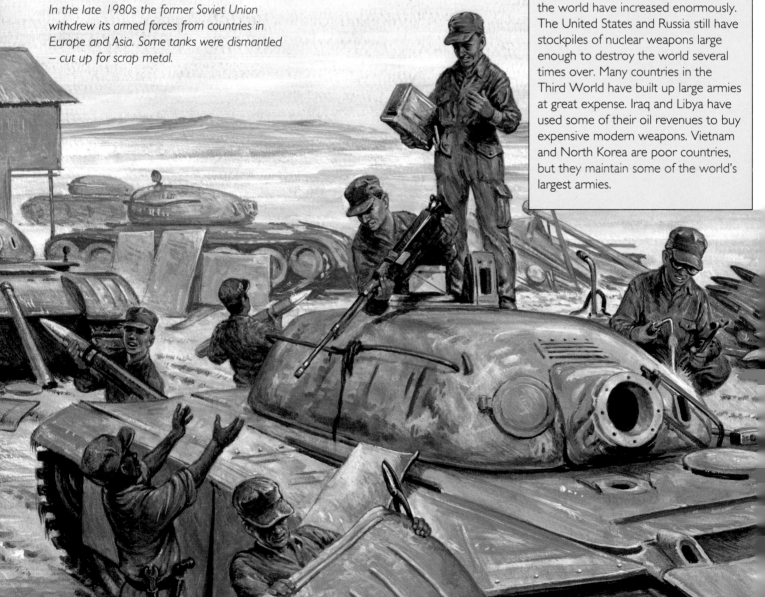

In the late 1980s the former Soviet Union withdrew its armed forces from countries in Europe and Asia. Some tanks were dismantled – cut up for scrap metal.

Russia began a programme of nuclear disarmament.

Since 1945 most wars and conflicts have taken place in the Third World, outside the two main power blocs. Some of these have been civil wars – wars within a country – that have resulted from attempts to overthrow a government, or from clashes over racial, tribal or religious differences.

Sometimes the United States or Soviet Union became involved, often on different sides, but without confronting each other directly. Sometimes they have invaded smaller countries, or supplied friendly states engaged in war with arms or military advisers.

In the Far East major wars were fought in Korea (1950–3) and Vietnam (1963–75). Both wars involved the United States as a combatant and mirrored the wider struggle between Communists and anti-Communists. In several African countries there have been civil wars connected with independence – such as those in Nigeria, Zaire, Angola, Mozambique and Zimbabwe.

Terrorism and the Middle East

In several European countries – notably Britain, Germany and Spain – terrorist groups made violent attacks against government property or personnel. Other terrorist activity in Europe, such as aircraft hijacking and bombing of airports, has its origin in the Middle East.

The Middle East has become a 'theatre' of continuous conflict, much of it related to the problem of finding a homeland for the Palestinian people. Israel went to war with its Arab neighbours in 1947, 1956, 1967, 1973 and 1982. Iraq and Iran fought a long and bloody war during the 1980s.

In 1991 the war between Iraq and the US-led United Nations coalition produced some of the biggest military operations since 1945.

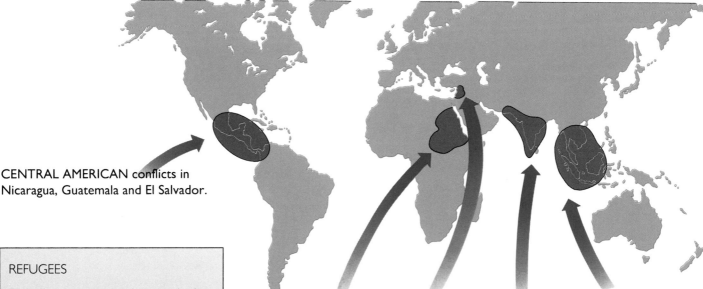

CENTRAL AMERICAN conflicts in Nicaragua, Guatemala and El Salvador.

REFUGEES

There has been a large increase in the number of refugees in the world in the last generation. Although it is difficult to say exactly how many, it is estimated that there are perhaps more than 15 million today worldwide. While many of these have left their country because of natural disasters such as floods or drought, others have fled from political and military conflicts. The breakup of Yugoslavia produced many thousand refugees in the 1990s.

AFRICA Wars in Somalia, Ethiopia, Sudan and Chad have displaced millions of people. Further south, more people have fled from wars in Angola and Mozambique.

MIDDLE EASTERN wars and conflicts, especially in Lebanon, Israel and Iraq. Millions of Kurdish and Shi'ite Muslim refugees fled to the Turkish and Iranian borders after the Gulf War of 1991.

INDIA, PAKISTAN AND AFGHANISTAN A third of the population of Afghanistan fled from the Soviet invasion of 1979 and the civil war which followed. This created a huge refugee problem for Pakistan.

SOUTH-EAST ASIA Thousands of Vietnamese 'boat people' fled across the water to Hong Kong, the Philippines and Indonesia. Thousands of Cambodian refugees live in camps in neighbouring Thailand.

Health and Education

Some of the biggest contrasts between rich and poor countries are in the fields of health care and education. Although the rich countries may spend a lot on these services, this is only a small proportion of their total wealth. Poorer countries often give priority to economic development, and have very little left to spend on the health and education of their people.

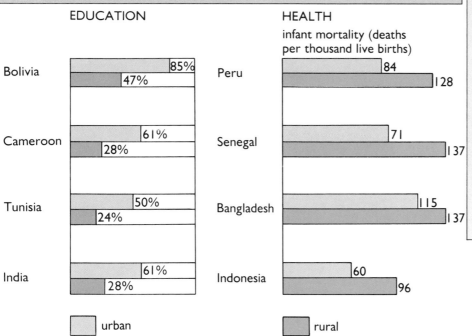

EDUCATION

Bolivia	85% (urban)	47% (rural)
Cameroon	61% (urban)	28% (rural)
Tunisia	50% (urban)	24% (rural)
India	61% (urban)	28% (rural)

HEALTH
infant mortality (deaths per thousand live births)

Peru	84 (urban)	128 (rural)
Senegal	71 (urban)	137 (rural)
Bangladesh	115 (urban)	137 (rural)
Indonesia	60 (urban)	96 (rural)

☐ urban   ☐ rural

Above: *Education and health in some of the world's poorer countries. People who live in rural areas are often worse off than those who live in towns.*

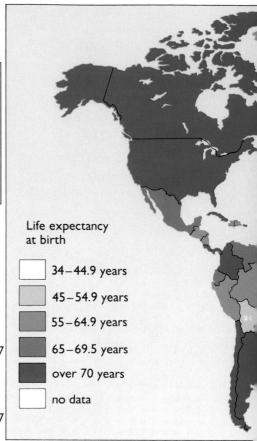

Life expectancy at birth

☐ 34–44.9 years
☐ 45–54.9 years
☐ 55–64.9 years
☐ 65–69.5 years
☐ over 70 years
☐ no data

Health care for poor and rich

All over the world most of the spending on health is directed towards curing illness rather than preventing it. The richer countries spend large sums on sophisticated equipment such as kidney machines, which bring relief to those in need but help only a few people. Even in the poorer countries such facilities are available to those who can afford to pay for them. By contrast much less is spent on 'primary' health care such as village clinics which, by making simple medical techniques available to a large number of people, could help to save many lives.

AN UNHEALTHY WORLD

Ill health affects an enormous number of people. For instance, some 500 million people, equivalent to a population the size of Western Europe, are partly blind with *trachoma*, an eye disease spread by unclean water and poor hygiene. Malaria infects 800 million people each year, and the number of sufferers at any one time is about 200 million – equivalent to the populations of Japan, Malaysia and the Philippines put together.

The industrialized world is much better off than the developing countries in all aspects of health care. In these countries, one in six children die in the early years of life and a further third of the population is affected by disability and disease. The main causes are lack of health workers, a shortage of drugs and vaccines, poor sanitation and shortage of clean water. Hunger and malnutrition also make people more vulnerable to disease. Compared with the United States, where there is, on average, one doctor for every 470 people, in Singapore one doctor is shared between 1,309 people and in Guyana between 9,600 people.

Yet although the richer, industrialized countries may spend up to ten times as much

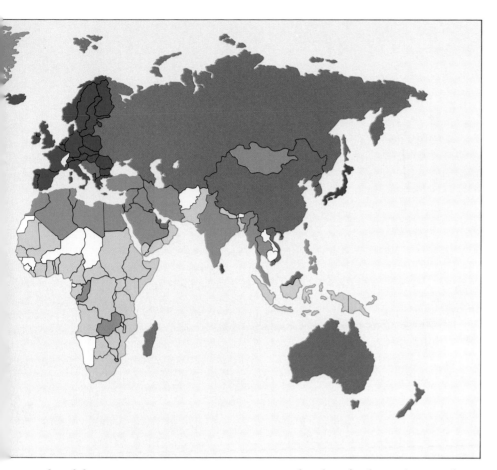

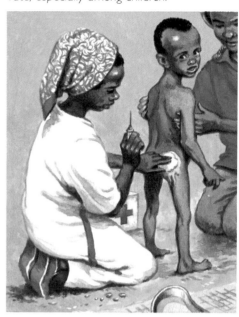

In Third World countries immunization programmes against infectious diseases such as smallpox are helping to reduce the death rate, especially among children.

on health care as poorer countries, their people are not always more healthy. The rapid pace of life is often stressful and many people suffer from diseases related to overeating, smoking and heavy drinking. Deaths from cancers and heart diseases have increased greatly in these countries in this century. Even so, the people there are living longer than they used to, and the elderly are making up a bigger proportion of the population. This means that the richer countries will need to spend still more on health care in the future.

Education and literacy

The difference in health care standards between rich and poor countries is matched by the difference between their standards of education and literacy (the ability to read and write). In most Third World countries only a small part of the population can read and write. European and African countries spend about the same share of their national wealth on education, but this means that about eight times as much is spent on a European child's education as on that of the average African. American children have 30 times as much spent on their education as African ones.

Illiterate people are always at a disadvantage. They may not be able to get a job, they may not know their rights as citizens, or know how to vote, and they cannot even read a newspaper. Illiteracy is a major problem for the poorest people of the poorest countries.

SOME SUCCESSFUL COUNTRIES

CHINA has over 1,000 million people, many of whom are among the world's poorest. Yet 66 per cent of the adult population can read and write. Moreover, a comprehensive health service has raised life expectancy to an average of 64 years. These achievements have been due to state planning and control, but the cost has been a curb on political freedom.

COSTA RICA is a small, Central American country with a higher quality of life than its neighbours. Its life expectancy, 70, is the second highest in Latin America, and the literacy rate is 90 per cent. But like many developing countries it is heavily in debt to the richer countries of the world.

DENMARK has one of the highest living standards in Europe, despite being one of its smaller countries. Its stable population has a 99 per cent literacy rate and a life expectancy of 75 years. Although Denmark is not a highly industrialized country, it provides for most of its own needs.

Women in the World

In many countries of the world women have for a long time enjoyed fewer rights and privileges than men. Often, they are poorer than men, are totally dependent on them, and have fewer opportunities for improvement or to develop the full potential of their capabilities. Some countries are now taking steps to reduce inequalities based on gender; others are resisting any change in the position of women, especially when it goes against the religious or cultural traditions on which the country's way of life is based.

The developed world

Traditionally, the woman's role has been to care for the home and bring up the children, while the man has gone out to work to earn a wage or salary in order to keep himself and his family.

This pattern is now changing, as in industrialized countries women make up an increasing proportion of people in employment. Almost 40 per cent of the workforce in the United States, Britain and Japan are women. It is often forgotten that women who stay at home are also working – in the United States the value of this invisible work makes up 40 per cent of the country's total wealth.

Generally, women are inadequately rewarded for the contribution they make to society. Those who are employed outside the home often have poorly paid jobs, work longer hours than men and receive lower wages. In the United States, women workers are paid, on average, 40 per cent less than male workers. They are also poorly represented in society. The map below shows that in most developed countries very few women are elected to parliaments or other bodies where decisions are made.

The developing world

In the developing world the position of women is far worse. It has been estimated that women do 70 per cent of all farm work. In Tanzania, for instance, women work an average of 2,600 hours per year in agriculture, compared with 1,800 hours for men. Besides this, they also run the home, care for the children and may spend several hours every day carrying water or collecting firewood. Yet, although they

The female voice in national legislatures (parliaments) is growing, but there are few women in positions of power in government. Women prime ministers have included (left to right) Indira Gandhi (India), Margaret Thatcher (Great Britain) *and* Golda Meir (Israel).

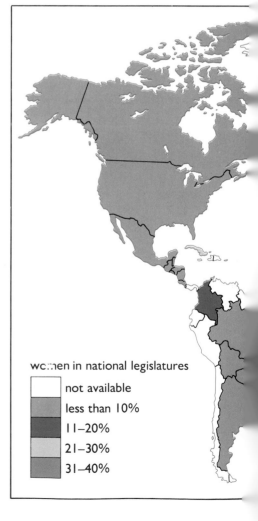

women in national legislatures

- not available
- less than 10%
- 11–20%
- 21–30%
- 31–40%

produce most of the food, women are more likely to be undernourished than men. The illiteracy rate among women is generally much higher than among men and educational opportunities are fewer. In Asia for every 100 boys in a school there are only 60 or 70 girls.

In many developing countries women have few rights as citizens. This is particularly true of some Islamic countries. In Saudi Arabia, for example, women are not allowed to be seen in public with their heads uncovered, and are forbidden to drive motor vehicles and to vote. Moreover, very few girls receive any education.

1 walking to field
2 ploughing, planting
3 collecting firewood
4 pounding grain
5 fetching water
6 lighting fire, cooking
7 serving food, eating
8 cleaning and washing

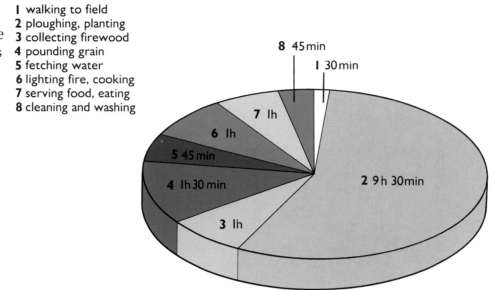

8 45 min
1 30 min
7 1h
6 1h
5 45 min
4 1h 30 min
3 1h
2 9h 30 min

Above: *The working day of a Zambian woman. In developing countries women not only look after homes but do much of the agricultural work as well.*

The voice of women

In recent years the call for women's rights has increased. In Scandinavian countries, and also in Russia and Cuba, women have had a share of political decision-making for many years. The United Nations Decade for Women, from 1975 to 1985, made more people aware of the problem of women's rights, and organizations to promote these rights have been formed in a number of countries.

In some countries women have taken direct action to make their voices heard. In Britain during the 1980s women maintained a demonstration for many years against the installation of cruise nuclear missiles from the United States. In Chile and Argentina groups of women protested against the arrest, imprisonment and, in many cases, total disappearance of relatives whose political views were opposed to the state.

Development and Aid

Many people in the world's poorer countries are trapped in a 'poverty cycle'. People living in poverty in the countryside sometimes try to break out of it by moving to the towns, but find that they are simply exchanging one kind of poverty for another. Even economic development or aid from richer countries is not always successful in overcoming poverty.

Kinds of development

It is often thought that the way for a country to break out of poverty cycles is by investing in projects which will further the country's development. To do this the country decides to borrow money from richer countries to spend on hydroelectric schemes, irrigation, roads, cities and industries. It is thought that as a result the country will be able to develop more industries, produce the food it needs, and market its products through an efficient transport system. Fewer imports will be needed and goods can be produced for export. It will soon be able to pay back the cost of the original loan.

Unfortunately this approach does not often work out. Many countries have found it hard to pay even the interest on the loans, and they have had to take out even bigger loans to pay off the original ones. They are now so hopelessly in debt that they cannot possibly hope ever to pay off what they owe to the richer nations. They have found that the benefits from the big projects have been slow to spread to the majority of the population.

Some countries are now coming to the conclusion that growth based on a few expensive projects may not be the answer anyway. They are looking instead at ways of development which use their own resources and make them less dependent on other countries. They are recognizing that it is often better to spend what they can afford on raising everybody's living standards by only a small amount, instead of borrowing to invest in big projects from which only a few people will benefit.

Aid to poorer countries

Aid is help given by richer countries to poorer ones. Some aid is in the form of money given directly by one government (the donor government) to another. 'Bilateral' aid is money which the receiving country must spend on goods and services from the donor country. 'Multilateral' aid is given by governments to international organizations such as the United Nations or the World Bank. This aid is then passed on to many different countries.

Voluntary organizations such as Oxfam and Christian Aid collect money from the general public. They spend much of what they raise on projects in developing countries, such as housing or agricultural schemes, or on

Below: Large-scale projects such as dams and hydroelectricity schemes keep countries in debt for many years.

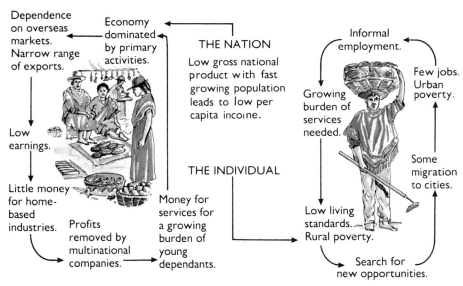

Dependence on overseas markets. Narrow range of exports.

Economy dominated by primary activities.

THE NATION
Low gross national product with fast growing population leads to low per capita income.

Low earnings.

Little money for home-based industries.

Profits removed by multinational companies.

Money for services for a growing burden of young dependants.

THE INDIVIDUAL

Informal employment.

Few jobs. Urban poverty.

Growing burden of services needed.

Some migration to cities.

Low living standards. Rural poverty.

Search for new opportunities.

Above: *The cycle of poverty. People who move from the countryside to the towns do not always become better off.*

aid may take the form of food, medical supplies, or equipment such as machinery and tractors. Aid also includes skilled people such as scientists, teachers, doctors and advisers.

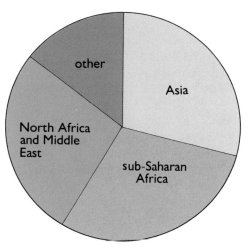

Where the aid goes. A lot of aid has been going to Africa and the Middle East, where entire populations have been facing starvation.

health and medical care. From time to time they have to raise additional funds to cope with specific emergencies such as the famines in Sudan and Ethiopia in the 1980s.

Aid takes many different forms. Besides financial help,

How useful is aid?

Although aid schemes bring some help to poor countries, many people question their real value. They say that the donor governments only give away what they don't need anyway, such as food surpluses. This is not always what the poor countries require. They also point out that aid sometimes fails to reach the people who need it because of the problems of transport or distribution. Some aid is stolen and sold for profit. Other people, however, say that without aid the populations of many poor countries would be even worse off.

Left: *Famine relief being distributed.*

References

Age structure The make-up of a population according to age. *See* **Population pyramid.**

Aid Help given to poor countries. This may include money, loans, food, project developments and expertise. Some aid is given to meet specific emergencies, such as famines and earthquakes. *See* **Bilateral aid** *and* **Multilateral aid.**

Bilateral aid Money given by rich to poor countries to be used to buy goods or services from the donor country.

Birth rate The number of births per thousand population per year.

'Boat people' Refugees from Communist Vietnam. They fled by boat to neighbouring Pacific countries after 1979, often enduring great hardship.

Cold War The political and military confrontation between the superpowers and their respective allies which lasted from 1945 until the end of the 1980s, but did not lead to war.

Death rate The number of deaths per thousand population per year.

Density of population The ratio of people to land, for example 100 persons per square kilometre.

Development Improvement in the social and economic conditions of a country. Development involves producing more wealth, raising the standard of living and creating a better quality of life.

Development gap The differences in the levels of development between countries. Many people believe that the gap between richer and poorer countries is widening.

Esperanto An artificial language, containing elements of other languages, intended as a universal language. It is spoken by about 100,000 people.

Ethnic Relating to the race or culture to which people belong.

Ethnic minority A population within a larger population, but with a different culture, religion, nationality or way of life.

Interdependence The view that the nations of the world depend on each other through trade, exchange of ideas and technology.

Iron Curtain The Cold War division between the Communist countries of Eastern Europe and the non-Communist countries of Western Europe. It came into being in the late 1940s and gradually disappeared with the revolutions in Eastern Europe in 1989–90.

Less developed country (or LDC) A country of the Third World.

Life expectancy The average age to which people can expect to live. Women normally have a slightly higher life expectancy than men.

Literacy Being able to read and write.

Migration The movement of people from one area, region or country to another. Some migrations are temporary or seasonal (eg nomadism), but others involve permanent settlement.

Multilateral aid Aid given from rich countries to a range of poor countries. It is often distributed through international aid organizations such as the United Nations.

'North' The developed, industrialized continents, most of which are in the northern hemisphere. *See* **'South'.**

Oil-rich country A country that depends for its wealth on the sales of oil (petroleum) to other countries. Most oil-rich countries are in the Middle East, for example Iran, Saudi Arabia, Kuwait, Iraq and the United Arab Emirates.

Overpopulation A condition in which population is too large for the resources (eg land) available to support it.

Population 'explosion' The very rapid rate of population increase which, it is feared, will lead to a situation in which the world will no longer be able to support all its people adequately.

Population projection An estimate of future population size, based on current size and population trends.

Population pyramid A diagram using a pyramid structure to show the different age groups in a population, and the proportion of males to females.

Poverty cycle The idea that poverty and poor living conditions lead to even more poverty. Once people become trapped in the poverty cycle they find it very hard to break out of it.

Primary health care The provision of simple, immediate cures for common ailments, for example at local clinics.

Refugee A person who cannot return to his or her own country because of fear of persecution or imprisonment.

Resource Something which can be used by people. A country's resources include its land, minerals, sources of power, skills of its people, etc.

Sex structure The make-up of a population according to the balance between males and females. *See* **Population pyramid.**

'South' The less developed continents, most of which are in the southern hemisphere. *See* **'North'.**

Third World The world's less developed countries (sometimes known as LDCs).

Underpopulation A condition in which the resources of an area or country could support a bigger population.

United Nations An international body which promotes world peace and cooperation. Most countries belong to it.

Westernization The spread of the way of life of Western Europe and North America to the countries of the Third World. It includes the spread of modern technology and often involves urban and industrial growth.

People and Homes

Rural Settlement

In many developing countries the majority of the population still live in rural settlements. A rural settlement may be a village, a group of houses, or a single house surrounded by countryside. In the developed world, most people live in towns or cities, and only a minority live in rural places.

Types of rural settlement

Villages are generally compact clusters of dwellings. In a nucleated village all the buildings form a tight group which defines the boundary of the built-up area. In a linear village, however, the buildings are strung out in a line along a road, river or valley. Hamlets are smaller villages, perhaps consisting of no more than half a dozen dwellings grouped around a road junction. There are many hamlets in Wales, the Pennines, and other hilly areas of Britain. Even smaller than the hamlets are the dispersed settlements. They include single farmhouses or cottages dotted over the landscape, with no village centre. The prairies of Canada and the United States, for instance, have many farms but no villages.

The inhabitants of some villages follow a common way of life. For example, in agricultural villages, most people own farms, work on the land surrounding the village, or provide some service to the agricultural community, such as the repair of farm vehicles and machinery. Mining and fishing villages are other examples of rural communities with a common interest or means of livelihood.

Changing village life

In many developed countries traditional village life is rapidly dying out. Increasingly, the villages are being taken over by better-off people who work in the town but prefer to live in the country. Often, they travel to work by car each day, and look to the towns for most of the services they need, including their children's education. Consequently, shops, post offices and schools are in decline and facing

Below: Nucleated, linear and dispersed settlements.

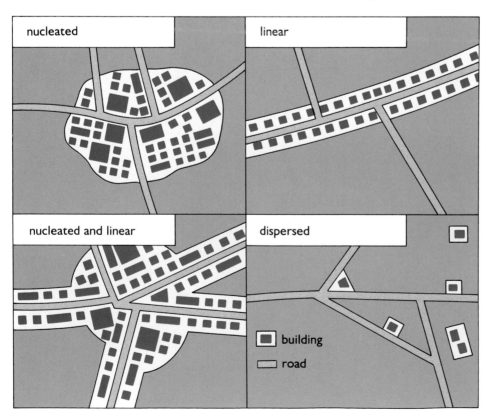

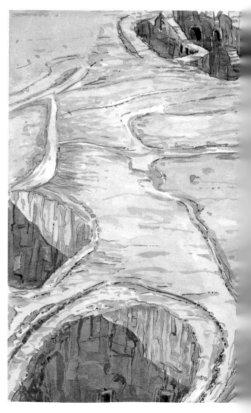

A traditional English village, built using local building materials. Such villages are now increasingly inhabited by people who work in towns. Sometimes there are no shops or any other local services.

HOUSES UNDERGROUND

Hundreds of years ago, at Matmata, in Tunisia, enormous round holes were dug in the mountainsides. The bottom of the hole acted as a courtyard, while smaller holes in the steep sides served as rooms. The courtyards were reached by long underground tunnels, making the homes secure from enemies.

closure. Many villages have become dormitory settlements for urban commuters, as local people are forced to leave because they can no longer afford to buy houses there. Sometimes new villages are built to house the surplus populations of nearby overcrowded cities.

In poor, developing countries, village life is also declining. Poverty in the countryside makes more people leave their villages for the city. In war-torn countries such as Mozambique, entire villages have been destroyed and rebuilt, only to be destroyed again in the course of the conflict.

Village housing

Traditional village housing varies a great deal because people use local materials and build to suit their particular needs. In the Karakoram mountains of north-west India and Pakistan the houses are made of massive boulders and timbers to withstand the frequent earthquakes experienced in the region.

The villagers of Benin, in west Africa, build their houses on lakes. First, poles are driven into the lake floor to support a platform on which the dwelling can be built.

In Saharan and Arab countries, such as Morocco or Yemen, wealthy farming families build houses of five or six floors with bricks made of sun-dried mud and straw. The family lives on the upper floors, the ground floor being used for storage or for keeping animals. In olden days the plan of the house helped protect families from desert bandits.

Urbanization

Urbanization is the growth of towns and cities. An urbanized country is one where most people live in towns and cities. Many countries in the developed world have an urban population of 80 per cent or more. Most developing countries are far less urbanized, but have rapid rates of urbanization. In the next generation or two, countries such as Venezuela could become more urbanized than Britain.

Migration to the cities

The growth of towns is often linked with industrial growth. Countries such as Britain, Germany and the United States became urbanized during the last century, as their industries grew and required more and more labour. Venezuela's industries have been expanding with the exploitation of its oil and mineral resources, and so has its urban population.

The greater security and higher wages offered by industrial employment is a major incentive that attracts people from country areas to cities. Other 'pull' factors include the expectation of better education, housing or medical care, and greater choice in life.

People also migrate to the cities because of the problems they find living in the countryside. In the Third World rural areas increasingly suffer from overpopulation, shortage of land on which to grow food, and poverty. Natural hazards such as typhoons or droughts can cause crop failure and famine in densely populated districts. Moreover, the greater use of machines in agriculture has reduced the need for farm labourers on estates and plantations. All these 'push' factors encourage people to look to the cities for a better way of life.

However, migrants to the cities also often suffer great disappointment. As more people move into the cities, so the demands on services such as housing, water and power supplies and health care

Below: Urban population as a proportion of total population in the United Kingdom, Italy and Venezuela.

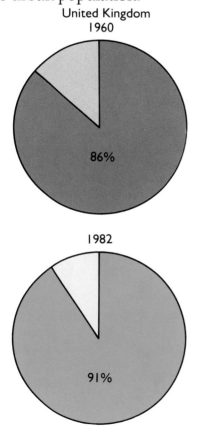

United Kingdom
1960

86%

1982

91%

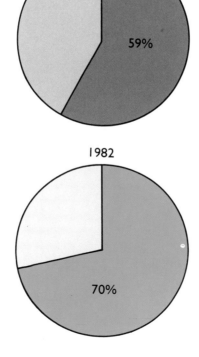

Italy
1960

59%

1982

70%

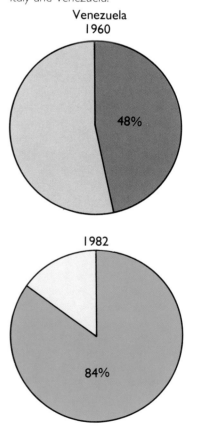

Venezuela
1960

48%

1982

84%

CONURBATION
A very large built-up area made up of towns or cities that have grown and merged.
Population about 0.5–1 million.
A huge range of all types of services.

CITY
A very big town, the most important in its area.
Population about 100,000–200,000.
A huge range of all types of services.

TOWN
Size varies with country.
Population about 2,000–10,000 minimum to 50,000–100,000 maximum.
Many services of different types.

VILLAGE
Up to several thousand people.
Only a few services, often with little choice.

HAMLET
A small village varying in size from 2 or 3 houses to about 100 people.
Often has no services at all.

stretch the limited resources available. Some cities become surrounded by shanty towns, built as temporary shelters, because there is no cheap housing. Furthermore, the number of jobs is much less than the number of people who want them, so migrants may remain unemployed and poor for many years.

Hierarchies of settlements

In the industrialized world, where countries have a long history of urbanization, there is a hierarchy or ranking of settlements within a region according to their size and importance. The most important type is the conurbation formed by several urban areas joining together to make one massive built-up area. Conurbations provide an enormous range of services

and employment, not just for themselves but also for the places outside.

Within the sphere of influence of the conurbation there may be many smaller nearby towns or villages. These will be partly or wholly dependent on the larger conurbation. For example, people may normally find everyday shopping in the town where they live, but will have to visit a larger city to find luxury items. The smallest settlements, including villages and hamlets, may have no services of their own at all, but depend entirely on bigger places for services and employment.

Shanty towns are often the only homes available to people in the Third World who migrate to the cities. A new one can spring up in just a few days.

City Centres

The city centre is the hub of the city's business activities, where large numbers of offices and shops are found. For this reason, it is known as its central business district, or CBD for short. Every city has its own CBD.

Features of the CBD

The CBD is easily identified on aerial photographs of cities by the many tall office blocks that dominate the skyline. Although the skyscraper blocks may adjoin lower buildings, these are older. The high price of land means that new office building takes place upwards in order to use land fully. The edge of this tall building zone usually marks the limit of the CBD.

A city centre can present many faces. By day it can be a bustle of activity, with thousands of office workers and shoppers thronging the streets around the office blocks. At night the same streets can be deserted, after the workers who commute to their offices by train, bus, car or tramway have all returned to their homes in the suburbs. The city centre is heavily used by people who come from outside, but very few people live there.

In very large cities different parts of the centre have a specialist character. Besides the main office blocks, there might be a shopping area with many department stores and chain stores selling luxury goods. Another part of the centre might be devoted to entertainments, with theatres, cinemas and restaurants. An older city will also have an area with many historic buildings, traditional shops and trades, and a much bigger resident population than the rest of the CBD.

Traffic congestion problems

Traffic congestion is a major problem in all city centres. Even though efficient public transport services are often available, many city streets are clogged with traffic throughout the day. To combat this, some cities try to limit the number of vehicles entering the centre and discourage on-street parking. Some city planners have concentrated new shopping areas in pedestrianized precincts, which have their own car parks and where shoppers can shop in more comfort.

Many American cities now offer only limited downtown (city centre) shopping facilities. Instead, the shops have all moved out of town to massive shopping complexes situated off the main highways. With easy parking and a huge range of goods all sold under one roof, shopping like this has its advantages provided that you have a car.

An architect's model of a central business district.

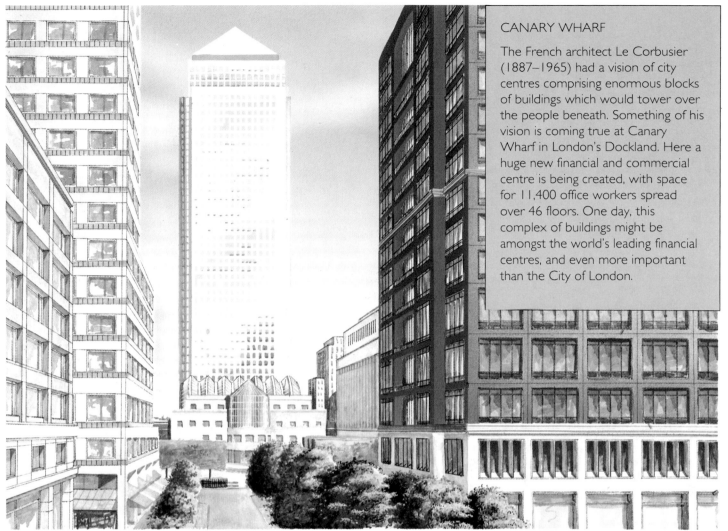

CANARY WHARF

The French architect Le Corbusier (1887–1965) had a vision of city centres comprising enormous blocks of buildings which would tower over the people beneath. Something of his vision is coming true at Canary Wharf in London's Dockland. Here a huge new financial and commercial centre is being created, with space for 11,400 office workers spread over 46 floors. One day, this complex of buildings might be amongst the world's leading financial centres, and even more important than the City of London.

TORONTO

Toronto is the principal city of Canada at the heart of a conurbation of some 3.1 million people. Like many North American cities, its downtown area (American for 'city centre') has a criss-cross layout. This includes specialized areas: a shopping zone centred on Queen Street/ Yonge Street crossroads, including theatres and other entertainments; a main office area to the west of the shopping area (one huge office block alone employs 60,000 people); Queen's Park, where administrative buildings, the university and hospitals are situated, and the harbour front and railway areas, where old industries exist alongside new leisure development schemes.

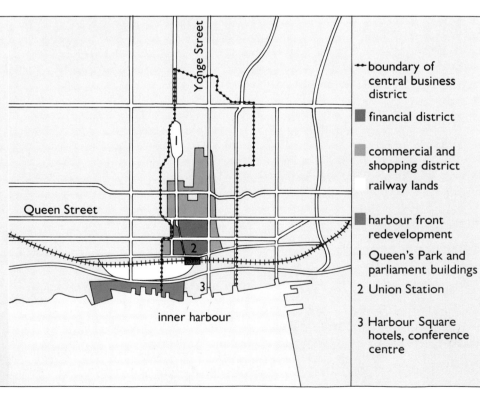

- ⟼ boundary of central business district
- ■ financial district
- ■ commercial and shopping district
- □ railway lands
- ■ harbour front redevelopment
- 1 Queen's Park and parliament buildings
- 2 Union Station
- 3 Harbour Square hotels, conference centre

Yonge Street

Queen Street

inner harbour

Two Contrasting Cities

The pictures on these pages show two sorts of city. One shows a city in a developed, industrialized country such as Britain. The other shows a city that is typical of a developing country. In both cities there are wealthy and poor areas.

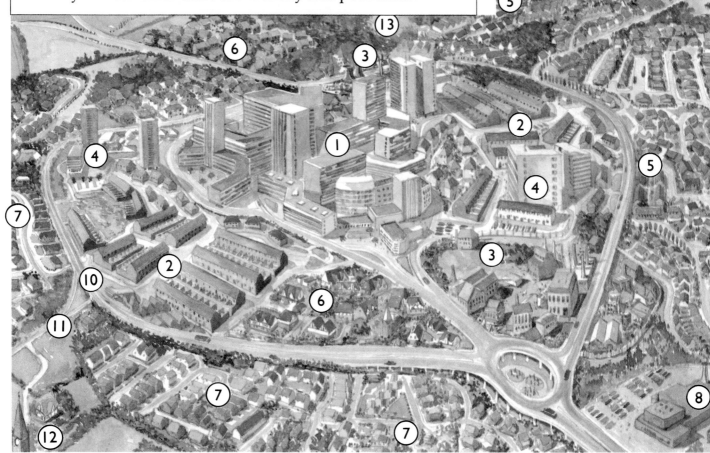

A BRITISH CITY

At the edge of the city centre (1), the tall office blocks give way to low cost housing dating from Victorian times. These are the inner suburbs or 'inner city' (2). Sometimes in need of repair, they are largely inhabited by poorer people, often the elderly or ethnic minority groups. Some of the houses in the inner city have been renovated and improved by better-off people. The inner city also includes older industrial neighbourhoods with industries which may be dying or have moved out of town (3). Some inner suburban areas have been cleared of older houses and redeveloped for high rise flats under modern housing schemes (4).

Further out from the city centre are the suburbs of more recent times. These include council-built housing estates (5) and houses built by private developers (6) and (7). Many of these houses are semi-detached (joined to the next house on one side) or detached (separate), with some modern terraces and bungalows. The newest houses are on the edge of the town. The most pleasant locations are likely to be taken up by the more expensive housing occupied by wealthy people.

The edge of the city also includes industrial estates or business parks (8). These are built for modern, light industries which depend on good road transport links. Like the big new out-of-town shopping centres (9), they are found close to motorways and major roads (10). Minor roads (11) link the city with villages which have expanded into dormitory settlements for commuters (12). Many who live here work in the city centre. The city is surrounded by a 'green belt' protecting it from further growth development (13).

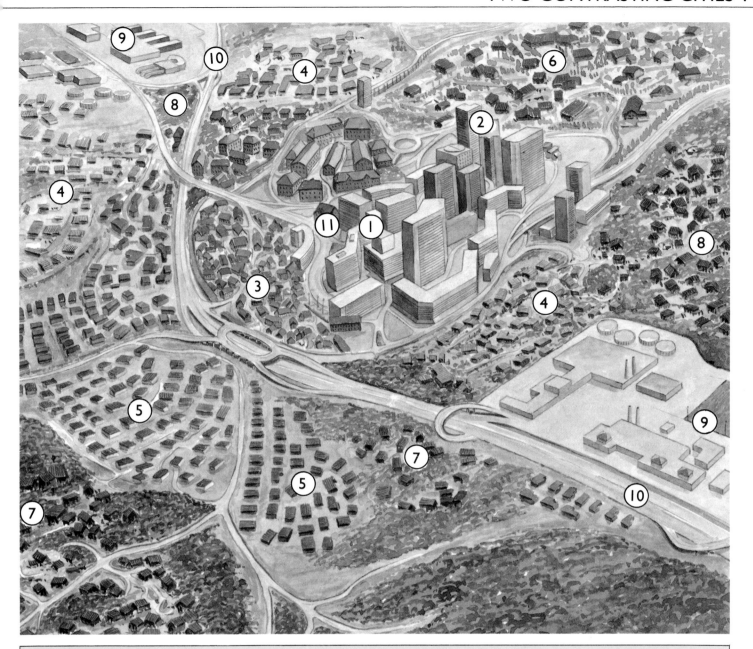

A CITY IN THE DEVELOPING WORLD

With its tall office blocks and modern shops and department stores (1), the centre is like that of any Western city. Not far away is the wealthy residential quarter, where the very rich, who govern the city and run its businesses, live in luxury apartments and flats (2). These people may see very little of the poorer parts of the city.

The modern city centre is next to the historic 'old' city of pre-colonial times (3). This has narrow, twisting streets, with traditional trades and markets, and perhaps still has its old city walls, built in bygone times to keep out invaders.

Adjoining the city centre are the districts where the urban poor live. The better off among them have permanent houses rebuilt out of former shanties, with basic amenities such as electricity and water from stand pipes (4). In other districts the government or city authority may be supporting self-help schemes to assist the poor to rebuild their housing areas themselves (5). These poorer areas contrast with the high quality suburban homes of the rich (6).

Most noticeable are the huge sprawling shanty towns of newly arrived migrants (7), often people with

no jobs and no prospects. The shanty towns quickly expand to fill areas of low-quality land (8). But the very poorest people have no homes at all, and live on the city streets.

The migrants hope to find jobs in the modern factories, often owned by foreign companies (9). Motorways built with foreign capital help these industries to distribute their products to other towns (10). Overcrowded buses carry the migrants into the city each day to look for work. Many migrants, however, live by selling, begging or scavenging on the streets (11).

World Cities

The number of very large cities across the world is growing. In 1950 there were only six cities with a population of more than five million, and they were all in the developed countries. By the end of the century there will be 50 cities of five million or more people, and 40 of them will be in the developing world.

Tokyo, Japan's super-city

Tokyo is Japan's capital – its 'super-city'. Today an international centre of finance and manufacturing, it grew rapidly during the postwar years (after 1945), when much of the city was rebuilt. The modern conurbation of Greater Tokyo includes 30 million people living within a 100-km (62-mile) radius.

A visitor to Tokyo describes the scene: "The houses press closer, until there are only inches between them. The roads, never wide, shrink to alleys down which even a miniature Japanese car cannot pass. Suburban railways run everywhere, with dowdy stations of steel girders and slabs of concrete, and rusty forests of bicycles parked outside. There are no parks, few playing fields, hardly a tree or touch of green, except in flowerpots or window-boxes. Nothing to look at but concrete walls, tin roofs, neon signs, a jungle of criss-crossed electric wires."

Tokyo has grown too fast for its planners, who now have to contend with enormous problems of traffic congestion and atmospheric pollution. A new plan for the city subtitled 'My Town Tokyo' aims to take into account what the ordinary people of Tokyo want their city to be like.

Sao Paulo, an industrial city

Sao Paulo is the largest city in Brazil and the capital of Sao Paulo state. In the 19th century it was the centre of the coffee

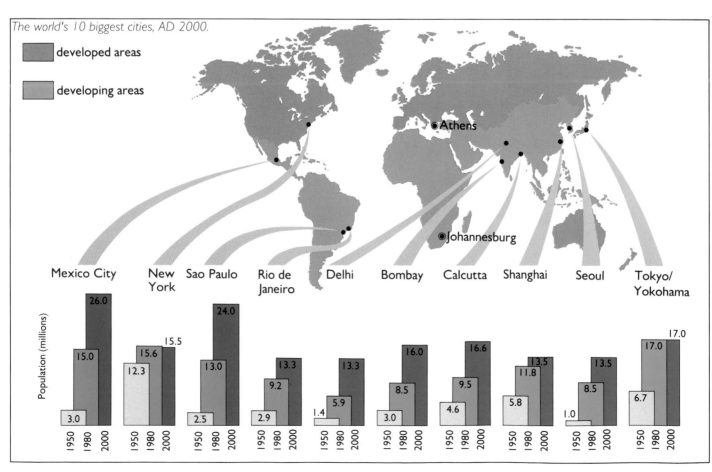

The world's 10 biggest cities, AD 2000.

- developed areas
- developing areas

Population (millions)

City	1950	1980	2000
Mexico City	3.0	15.0	26.0
New York	12.3	15.6	15.5
Sao Paulo	2.5	13.0	24.0
Rio de Janeiro	2.9	9.2	13.3
Delhi	1.4	5.9	13.3
Bombay	3.0	8.5	16.0
Calcutta	4.6	9.5	16.6
Shanghai	5.8	11.8	13.5
Seoul	1.0	8.5	13.5
Tokyo/Yokohama	6.7	17.0	17.0

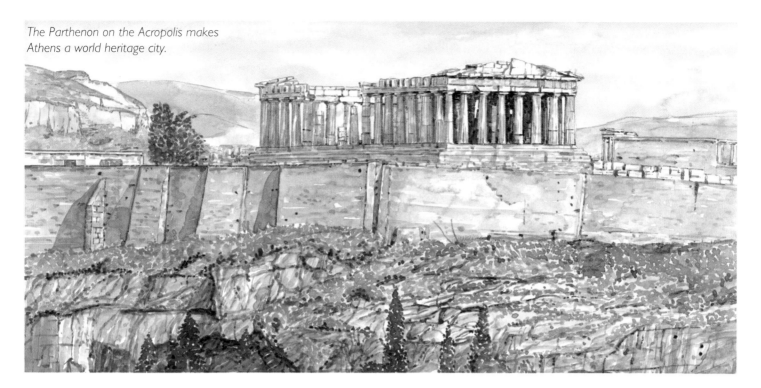

The Parthenon on the Acropolis makes Athens a world heritage city.

trade and became known as the 'coffee capital' of Brazil. In the present century it has been called the 'Chicago of South America' because of the rapid growth of its industries. Every year its population increases by some 500,000 and it spreads to occupy a further 60 square kilometres (23 square miles) of land.

Although very prosperous, Sao Paulo shows huge variations in wealth. The rich live in exclusive apartment areas while the poor inhabit *favelas* or shanty towns, which sprawl over much of the city.

Johannesburg, a divided city

Johannesburg, a city of 1.7 million people, is smaller than the super-cities shown on the map. It was founded in 1886 and grew quickly as the centre of the South African gold mining industry. Today it is South Africa's main commercial centre. The city

is overlooked by the spoil heaps from the gold mines.

A visitor describes how, over many years, the government policy of apartheid – the separation of racial groups – has affected Johannesburg: "There is a black majority on the streets, but officially it is classed as a white city, with most of its hotels, restaurants, bars, theatres, cinemas and other facilities reserved for whites only. About a million blacks, many of whom crowd the city's offices and shops by day, move back to the darkness of Soweto at night."

Soweto was built as a dormitory town for the black workers of Johannesburg. It has great overcrowding, few opportunities for leisure, and much unemployment. It has become a centre of political unrest and protest against the apartheid system, which is now gradually being dismantled.

Athens, a heritage city

Athens, the capital city of Greece, has a population of 3.7 million. Far older than Tokyo, Sao Paulo or Johannesburg, it is a 'world heritage' city in which modern urban development is overlooked by monuments from the ancient Greek civilization. The most famous of these is the Parthenon, built 2,500 years ago on the hill called the Acropolis.

Today the heritage of Athens is threatened by the modern world. Air pollution and the vibration from heavy traffic are causing the monuments to crumble very rapidly. If nothing is done about it, ancient carvings will soon be unrecognizable. If that happens, it will not just be Athens that is the loser; great monuments like the Acropolis are considered to belong not only to Greece but to the whole world.

Planned Towns and Cities

Often, older towns and cities grew up without any planning. New building took place wherever there was land available, with little control from planning laws or building regulations. Today, however, almost all countries try to contain urban growth. Many countries have tackled the problem of urban expansion by building entirely new towns and cities.

New towns in Britain

Britain has built 24 new towns since 1945, and has expanded a further six older towns into 'new' ones. Some new towns, for example Stevenage, in Hertfordshire, and Bracknell, in Berkshire, were built to rehouse people from older areas of large cities such as London. Others, such as Washington, in Tyne and Wear, were created to revive old, depressed industrial areas. The early new towns had 'target' populations of around 100,000, but some of the later ones were planned to be bigger. Milton Keynes, in Buckinghamshire, the largest, is intended eventually to have 200,000 inhabitants.

All the new towns are carefully planned, with pedestrianized shopping centres and easy access to the residential parts of the town. The residential areas are built on a 'neighbourhood' principle, each neighbourhood having its own shops, health centre and primary school. Factories and other industrial works are located on separate industrial estates. All housing areas have parks and open spaces nearby.

Jubail, a new industrial city on the Persian Gulf.

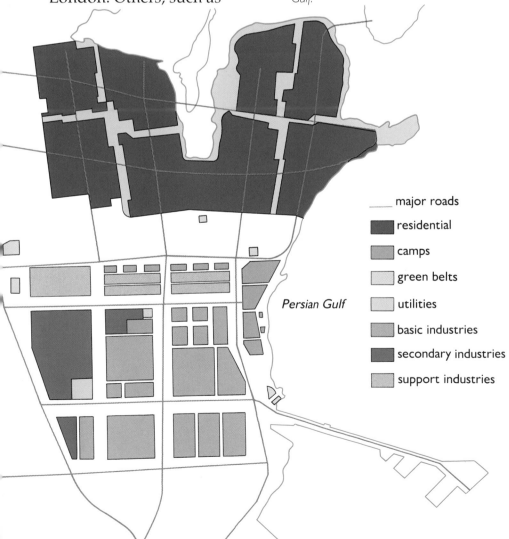

major roads
residential
camps
green belts
utilities
basic industries
secondary industries
support industries

Persian Gulf

New towns in the Middle East

Very different from Britain, Egypt, in the Middle East, has also tried to meet population needs by building new towns and cities. A fifth of Egypt's population of 51 million people live in Cairo, the capital, and their numbers are growing. The city already has vast housing estates stretching out into the desert, but the fertile plain of the Nile on which Cairo stands is too valuable to be built upon. Consequently, 19 new towns are being built which, it is intended, will take two million people by the year 2000. One of these new towns called Tenth of Ramadan City, is 80km (50 miles) north-east of Cairo in the desert. However, it is proving difficult to persuade people to leave Cairo and settle there. Even many of those who work in Tenth of Ramadan's new industries still prefer to commute from Cairo. The Egyptian government reckons that it will require a further 10 new towns, on top of the 19 being built, if it is to keep pace with its housing needs into the next century.

Saudi Arabia, another Middle Eastern country, is building new cities to further industrial development. For instance, at Yanbu, on the Red Sea, where there are major crude oil and gas processing plants, a city is being built to accommodate 150,000 people. The intention is to encourage the development of new industry that does not depend on oil, looking ahead to the

London's green belt is coming under intense pressure for developments for all purposes.

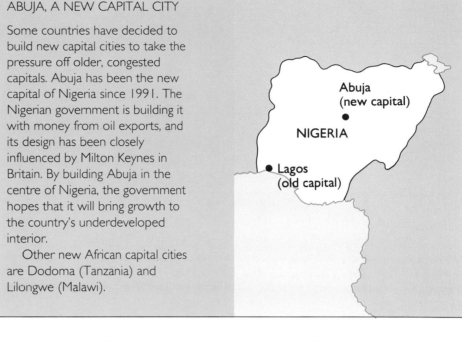

ABUJA, A NEW CAPITAL CITY

Some countries have decided to build new capital cities to take the pressure off older, congested capitals. Abuja has been the new capital of Nigeria since 1991. The Nigerian government is building it with money from oil exports, and its design has been closely influenced by Milton Keynes in Britain. By building Abuja in the centre of Nigeria, the government hopes that it will bring growth to the country's underdeveloped interior.

Other new African capital cities are Dodoma (Tanzania) and Lilongwe (Malawi).

time when Saudi Arabia's oil wealth might run out. Another industrial city for 270,000 is taking shape at Jubail on the Persian Gulf.

shopping

roads

industry

houses

LONDON

leisure

hotels

offices

□ original green belt

■ extensions since mid 1970s

airport

technology parks

Megalopolis
The massive, sprawling built-up area that results when a large city merges with surrounding towns is called a megalopolis. In the United States planners have given the name Boswash to the almost continuous urban area stretching for 700km (over 400 miles) along the east coast from Boston to Washington. The Boswash megalopolis includes New York, with a population of 11 million, and many other towns and cities. A similar super-conurbation, called Sansan, is appearing on the Californian coast between San Francisco and San Diego.

A megalopolis can cause major problems for planners. In Britain planners have tried to contain the growth of London and some other major cities by imposing curbs on the development of surrounding green belt land, but pressures for further growth are considerable.

References

Apartheid The South African government policy of separating white, black and 'coloured' (other non-white) peoples. Apartheid made people live in certain areas according to their race, and use separate amenities such as hospitals, schools, cinemas and buses.

Central business district (CBD) The central part of a town or city, including its offices, shops and entertainment areas.

Conurbation A large, continuously built-up urban area formed by the merging of towns or cities.

Counterurbanization The movement of people and businesses from cities and large urban centres to smaller towns and outlying centres.

Dormitory settlement A village inhabited by people who work in nearby towns and cities; they return home to the village in the evening and at weekends.

Downtown American for city centre.

Favelas Name for the temporary, makeshift homes of shanty towns in Brazil, South America.

Gentrification The renovation of older residential properties in inner city areas as they become fashionable districts once more. *See* **Inner city.**

Ghetto A residential area, usually in the inner city, mostly populated by one ethnic group. Ghettos are often areas of overcrowding, poor housing conditions and high unemployment.

Green belt A belt of land surrounding a town or city which is intended to protect it from any further building developments.

Grid layout Pattern of roads and streets crossing each other at right angles.

Hamlet A very small settlement. A hamlet is usually a cluster of buildings, but provides few or no services.

Hierarchy of settlement The division of settlements in a region into groups according to their size and the number and range of services they provide.

Hinterland *See* **Sphere of influence.**

Inner city The zone of a city surrounding the centre; a zone of older, often run-down property or industry and derelict land. Many parts of inner cities have been redeveloped.

Megalopolis An almost continuous built-up area made by the merging of several cities and towns. The built-up sections may be separated by tracts of open space such as parks, commons or golf courses.

Metropolis A very large urban area in which a major city becomes joined with neighbouring smaller cities or 'satellite' towns.

Millionaire city An urban area with a population of more than a million.

New town A planned town, often intended to rehouse people from nearby towns and cities. In Britain, a town built under the New Towns Act of 1946.

Nucleated settlement A compact form of settlement where the houses cluster around a central point, such as a road junction, church or pond.

Primate city The largest city of a country, not necessarily its capital.

Push and pull factors 'Push' factors are those, such as drought or famine, which influence people to leave their homes in rural areas; 'pull' factors are those which attract them to living in cities, such as better prospects of employment.

Rapid transit A public transport scheme for moving large numbers of commuters into and out of cities, for example, an underground railway system.

Rural Relating to the countryside.

Self-help scheme A housing project organized by the local community. The work is carried out by the residents themselves.

Settlement A place where people live. Farms, hamlets, villages, towns and cities are all settlements. Caravan parks and camping sites can be regarded as 'temporary settlements'.

Shanty town An area of very poor-quality housing on the edge of a Third World city. Dwellings are often made of cardboard, oil drums, tyres or other improvized scrap materials. Shanty towns are known variously as *favelas* (Brazil), *barriadas* (Peru), *bustees* (Calcutta) and *gecekondu* (Ankara, Turkey).

Sphere of influence The area served or influenced by a settlement, such as the area for which it provides services and employment.

Suburbanization The movement of people and businesses from inner urban areas to more outlying parts of the town or city.

Suburbs The residential areas of towns and cities. 'Suburbia' usually describes the more modern outer suburbs which lie beyond the inner city.

Urban Relating to towns and cities.

Urban renewal An attempt to improve the conditions of poor inner city areas by new planned building schemes, including housing, industries, shopping centres, etc.

Urban sprawl The unplanned spread of housing and other building developments at the edges of towns and cities, often outwards along main roads.

Urbanization The increasing proportion of a population living in urban areas.

Village A small settlement, larger than a hamlet but smaller than a town. Villages may be nucleated (ie compact) in shape, linear (along both sides of a single road) or dispersed (a scatter of dwellings). Villages usually provide only a small number of services for their residents.

People at Work

Hunting and Fishing

Hunting and fishing are the oldest known ways of making a living. Together with food gathering – the collection of fruits, berries and nuts – they were the only methods known to primitive peoples. Even today some communities partly depend on these activities for their survival, but very few peoples rely on them solely. They are examples of 'primary' activities, or livelihoods which use the Earth's resources at first hand.

Above: *Xingu Indians, hunting in the Amazon rain forest.*

Hunting

The Amazon rain forests of Brazil are some of the few remaining areas where hunting and food gathering are still the only way of life for local communities. Indian tribes such as the Xingu hunt the wild pig for food, catch fish from the many rivers, and collect wild fruit and nuts. They also grow crops such as manioc, maize and yams in forest clearings. The Xingu find all that they need for making their homes, weapons, clothes and tools from the forest around them.

Unfortunately the way of life of peoples like the Xingu is rapidly disappearing and even their survival is threatened, as more of the Brazilian rain forest is cleared away. The plight of forest tribes has attracted international attention and there have been calls for their protection. However it seems unlikely that their way of life can be saved.

Fishing

Fishing is a principal livelihood for many people who live on coasts, lakes or rivers. In Third World countries, where meat is scarce and expensive, fish is a major source of protein. In China and South-east Asia villagers have developed 'aquaculture', the rearing of fish in local ponds. A typical pond is well organized, with carp occupying the upper and middle levels of the pond and feeding off water plants and plankton (microscopic floating organisms), and dace occupying the lower levels. The pond forms part of the village agricultural system: it is fed with vegetable waste from the fields, and it supplies dredged sludge from the pond bottom for use as farm fertilizer.

Below: *Local fishermen, who work along the coast of the Bay of Bengal in India, using a purse seine net.*

Commercial fishing

Most of the world's fish catch comes from the oceans and depends on the use of modern large-scale methods. The principal oceanic fisheries are on the continental shelves, where penetrating sunlight warms the waters to create the food that the fish need. Much of the catch is taken by a small group of nations headed by Japan and Russia.

Japan alone catches 12 million tonnes of fish a year and employs some 500,000 people in fishing and related industries. Although three-quarters of Japan's catch comes from local waters, the Japanese also fish as far away as the North Atlantic and Antarctica.

There is increasing evidence that the oceans are being overfished. With modern fishing methods, fish are being removed from the oceans more quickly than they can be restocked by natural means. In recent years herring stocks have fallen by 40 per cent, and halibut by as much as 90 per cent. The situation for some other marine species is even worse. The larger whales, for instance, have been hunted almost to extinction.

Below: A modern trawler.

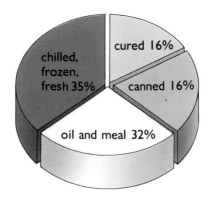

Above: *How the marine fishing catch is used.*
Right: *The world's main fishing grounds are on the continental shelves.*

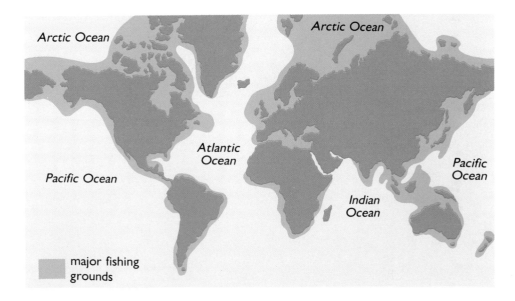

World Agriculture

The most important type of primary activity is agriculture, which employs more people worldwide than any other form of livelihood. However, most of these people are in the Third World. In many countries of Western Europe as few as two or three per cent of the population is engaged in farming, compared with more than 80 per cent in many Asian and African countries.

Types of farming

In arable farming the main activity and source of income is growing crops. Farming based on animal products, such as wool or meat, is called pastoral farming. Some farms are 'mixed', that is, they are concerned with both arable and pastoral farming. Some

Types of agricultural systems. Most farms fall within this scheme of classification.

farms are very specialized, concentrating on one product only, such as wheat, cattle (beef or dairy), sheep or fruit.

Subsistence farms are those that produce food and raw materials for the people who work on them. Commercial farms sell their produce to provide a cash income. Some farms are both subsistence and commercial, the farmers depending on the food they

grow but also producing some crops to be sold for cash.

Farming is classified according to how the land is used. Intensive farms are often small, but the outputs per worker and per unit area are high. This is because the ground is thoroughly worked, sometimes with the aid of machinery and chemicals, but often just by human and animal labour. Extensive farms are usually bigger. The ground is less productive and the yields per unit area are low, but the total output is often relatively large.

Tropical farming

Agriculture in the tropics includes both subsistence and commercial farming. Rain forests were traditionally farmed by 'shifting cultivation'. This involves clearing forest

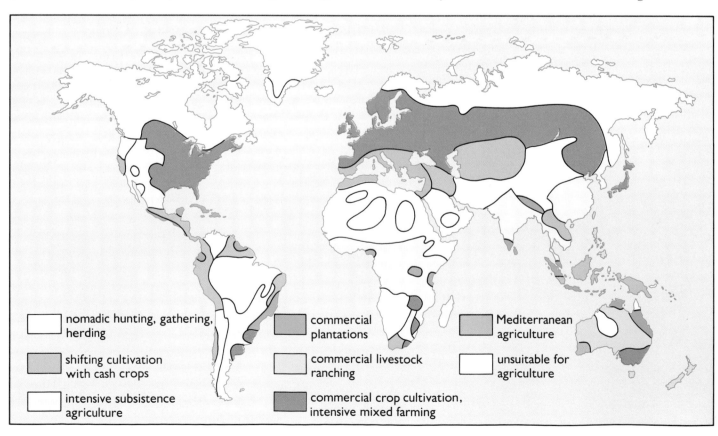

- nomadic hunting, gathering, herding
- shifting cultivation with cash crops
- intensive subsistence agriculture
- commercial plantations
- commercial livestock ranching
- commercial crop cultivation, intensive mixed farming
- Mediterranean agriculture
- unsuitable for agriculture

AGRICULTURAL SYSTEMS			
Main land	Main function	Main scale of use	Some examples
ARABLE	subsistence	intensive	Peasant farms, eg Indian rice farms
		extensive	Shifting cultivation, bush fallowing
	commercial	intensive	Market gardening, horticulture, polder farms, bush fallowing
		extensive	Commercial cereal and prairie farms, plantations
MIXED	subsistence	intensive	Crofting types, some tropical peasant farms
		extensive	Nomadic pastoralists using rented grazings
	commercial	intensive	Temperate mixed farms of Europe, USA corn belt farms
		extensive	Cereal/livestock farms of pampas type grassland
PASTORAL	subsistence	intensive	Sedentary pastoralists of East Africa
		extensive	Nomadic pastoralists
	commercial	intensive	Grassland dairy farms
		extensive	Ranching, hill sheep farms
SPECIAL	commercial	arable	Glasshouse cultivation, floriculture, hop farming
		pastoral	Factory livestock units, poultry farms, urban farms

The distribution of main farming types. Within each category there may be many variations.

areas, cultivating them for a time before they become infertile, and then moving on to clear a fresh patch. There is little true shifting cultivation now, and most tropical peasant farmers combine settled subsistence farming with the growing of cash crops such as cocoa and groundnuts for export.

In areas with monsoon climates, rice is the dominant crop. It is grown very intensively, especially on wet valley floors and in deltas, where two crops a year are common. In savanna areas, with dry seasons, crop-growing is confined to wetter regions along river valleys or around water-holes, while the drier regions are given over to nomadic herding. Throughout the tropics cash crops are grown for export on large estates, called plantations.

Temperate farming
Warmer subtropical areas, such as the Mediterranean countries, support a mixed agriculture of grain, fruit and livestock farming, with both subsistence and commercial elements. In temperate regions with a continental-type climate, former grasslands have been converted to extensive wheat-growing regions, especially in Russia, Ukraine and North America. Drier grassland areas are used for livestock ranching.

Farming the wetter temperate parts of Europe and North America is very intensive and mechanized in order to meet the huge demand. The produce includes grain, fruit, vegetables, meat and dairy products, besides plants cultivated in glasshouses. Pigs and poultry are raised on 'factory farms' to maximize production.

Agricultural Products

Although most farmers live in the developing 'South', particularly in its tropical areas, most agricultural production is in the temperate areas of the 'North'. Only the industrial countries have the capital to invest in modern scientific and technological methods of farming. Many Third World farmers have to depend on older, traditional methods.

Cereals

Wheat provides a staple crop for over a third of the world's population. It is the most important grain crop of the temperate regions, and is also important (sown in autumn for harvesting the next year) in monsoon areas. The main producers are Russia, Ukraine, the United States, Canada and China. China is also one of the main rice producers. Rice is the leading tropical crop in Asia and is a highly nutritious food. It is cultivated on flood plains to feed densely populated areas. India and Indonesia are other main producers.

Maize is a staple crop in South America and Africa and is fed to animals in the United States. The United States and China are the leading producers. Other important cereal crops are barley, oats and rye in temperate regions, and millet (sorghum) in the drier parts of Africa and Asia.

Other food crops

In moist temperate regions, potatoes are an important food crop, especially in Europe and China. Other major root crops include yams (sweet potatoes) in wetter tropical regions, and cassava, a drought-resistant vegetable which is very important in Africa. Sugar beet is a main source of sugar in European countries.

Some tropical crops are grown mainly as cash crops for export. These include tea, from India and China; cacao, grown in west Africa and exported to make cocoa and chocolate; and coffee, produced in South America (notably by Brazil and Colombia) and in Africa. Other cash crops are sugar cane, from India, Brazil and Caribbean countries; soya beans, from the United States and Brazil; and ground nuts, from India. Soya beans and ground nuts are used as food crops and are made into vegetable oils.

Industrial crops

Non-food crops grown for export include cotton and rubber. Cotton grows in wet subtropical areas, especially in China, the United States, India and Pakistan. Rubber is a tree crop that is harvested in tropical rain forest areas such as in Malaysia, Indonesia and Thailand.

The world's main cereal-growing areas.

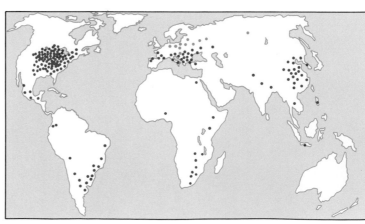

Animal products

Beef cattle are reared for meat. The United States and Europe provide beef for their own consumption, while Australia, New Zealand and Argentina produce beef which goes into world trade. Dairy cattle are raised for milk products, such as butter, yogurt and cheese, reared close to densely populated areas in North America and Western Europe. Australia and New Zealand are major contributors to world trade in dairy products. Sheep are raised for both wool and meat, mainly in Australia, New Zealand, Russia and China. Pigs, similarly, have a wide distribution, with large numbers in China, the North American corn belt, Europe and Russia.

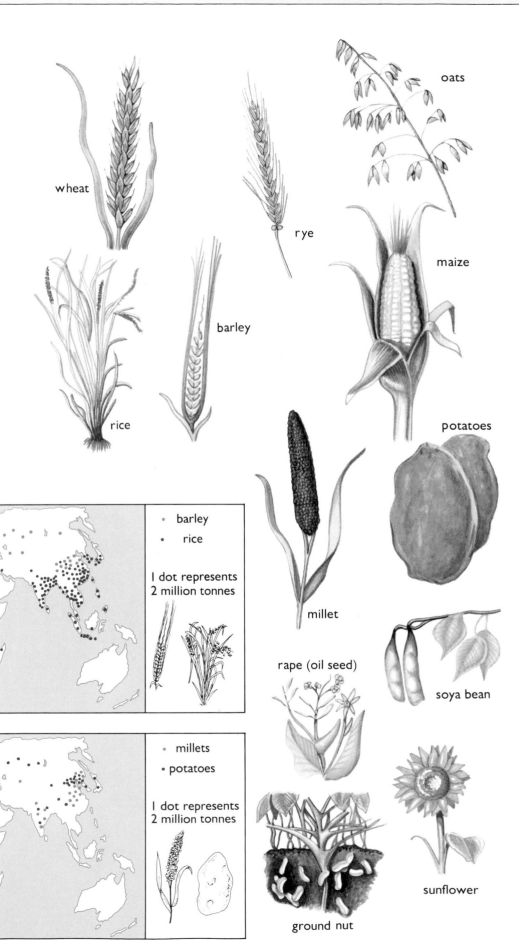

wheat

rye

oats

maize

barley

rice

millet

potatoes

rape (oil seed)

soya bean

ground nut

sunflower

- barley
- rice

1 dot represents 2 million tonnes

- millets
- potatoes

1 dot represents 2 million tonnes

Food for All?

Nearly 200 years ago, the economist Thomas Malthus predicted that a time would come when the population of the world would be so great that it could no longer feed itself. Since then the world's population has increased many times, but there is still enough food for the world as a whole. The problem is one of distribution. Many people in the developed countries consume more than they need while others in the Third World go hungry.

Agricultural improvement
Since Malthus' time there have been changes which have enabled world food production to keep pace with population growth. In the 19th century vast new lands were brought into cultivation, especially in Russia and North America, while during the 'agricultural revolution' in Europe new machinery and better farming techniques were introduced

The many ways in which farming can be made more productive. Some of these methods, however, bring environmental problems.

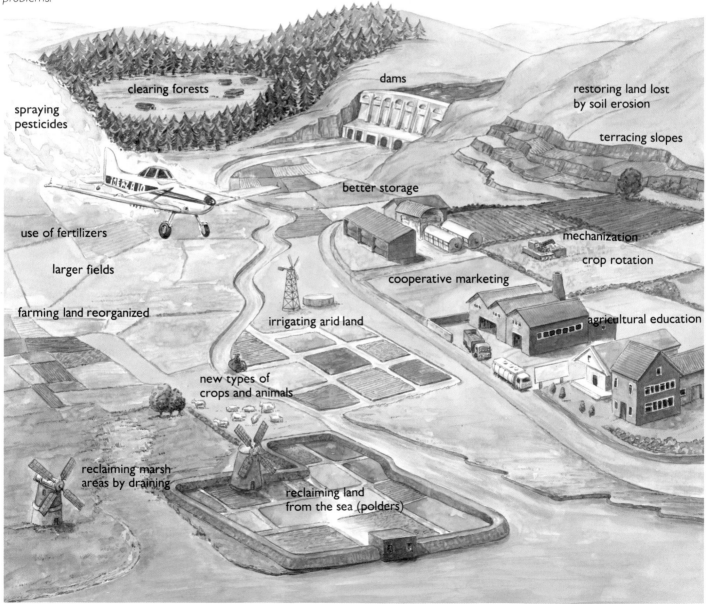

which gradually spread throughout the industrialized world. The present century has seen a new 'agricultural revolution' based on chemicals, artificial fertilizers and scientific farming which has enabled the developed countries to increase their food production yet further.

The 'Green Revolution'

For many years scientists have pinned their hopes of producing more food on the spread of technological farming to the Third World. Farmers using older, traditional methods have been encouraged to reorganize their land, consolidating it into larger blocks which can be more easily worked by large machines. They have also been urged to use new scientifically-produced seeds which give higher yields than those they collect from their own plants, and to buy artificial fertilizers,

The Green Revolution aims to help farmers to produce more food and to break out of the cycle of poverty into a cycle of higher living standards.

instead of using their own animal manure, so that the land can be cropped more intensively. They have further been persuaded to buy chemical pesticides and insecticides to control pests and diseases and improve the quality of the crop.

It was hoped that by using these methods, farmers would be able to break out of the 'vicious cycle of decline' into a 'growth cycle' which will improve living standards in the countryside and provide more food for sale.

In some ways the Green Revolution has been quite successful. Much land in developing countries has been made more productive, especially where the changes were well planned, properly supported by governments, and coordinated with the irrigation schemes on which they heavily depend. However, there have also been costly failures. Deforestation and overcropping caused soil erosion; the reorganization of farms has led to many small farmers losing their land and

The 'miracle' seeds of the Green Revolution must have an abundant and carefully controlled water supply. Traditional methods of irrigation are not always adequate.

being forced to look for work in the towns; and poor countries have become more dependent on the wealthier countries from which they buy their seeds and chemicals.

Alternative ways

Some people believe that the world food problem could be dealt with more effectively by other means. People in the developed countries, they say, consume more than their fair share of food and, in particular, depend heavily on meat in their diets. To produce this meat, a large part of the world's cereal production is used as animal feed, which is wasteful and an inefficient way of using protein. If those people ate less meat but more vegetables instead, it would be possible to grow more food for others.

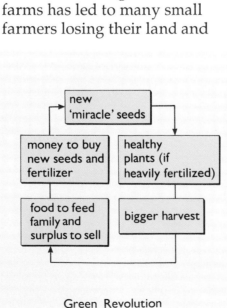

vicious cycle   Green Revolution

Mining

Mining is a primary activity – that is, one which supplies mineral resources to manufacturing industry. Different minerals have proved useful at different times in history. Stone Age people would have found no use for petroleum or uranium, just as people today have little use for the flint chippings from which Stone Age tools and implements were made.

Types of minerals

One variety of minerals are the fossil fuels. They include coal, petroleum (oil) and natural gas, which were formed organically over millions of years, from the remains of animals and plants. Fossil fuels are used to produce heat and energy, especially on a large scale in power stations.

Metallic minerals are formed when igneous material in cracks or veins in rock solidifies as it cools. The mineral bodies containing the metal are known as ores. Metallic minerals, especially the ores of iron, aluminium, copper, lead and zinc are vital to manufacturing industry.

Some minerals are precious. They include both metallic substances, such as gold and silver, and non-metallic ones, such as diamonds. Gold is especially important in world currency markets, as a measure of wealth.

Other minerals, called evaporites, are the deposits left behind when water evaporates from lakes rich in salts. Sulphur, gypsum and anhydrite are examples. They are all widely used in the chemical industry.

Certain minerals, such as uranium (for nuclear energy), have become important only in recent times. Others may have been used for a long time but have recently found new uses, for example silica, in the electronics industry. Building stones, sand, clay and gravel are found in quarries rather than mines.

Types of mining

Minerals at or very close to the surface can be extracted by open cast working, in which the surface layers are stripped away and then the minerals are dug out with large excavators. Deeper ores, or those lying in veins, have to be mined underground. Sometimes sloping tunnels, called drifts, can be driven

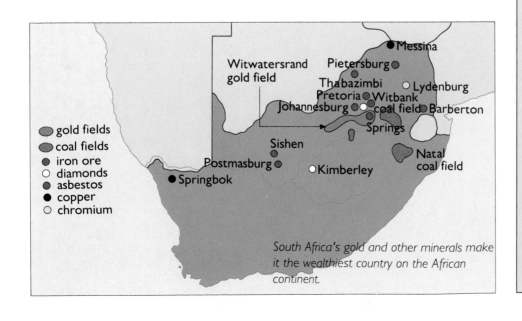

- gold fields
- coal fields
- iron ore
- diamonds
- asbestos
- copper
- chromium

South Africa's gold and other minerals make it the wealthiest country on the African continent.

PRINCIPAL MINERALS AND MINING PRODUCTS, AND HOW THEY ARE USED			
Use	Industries	Nature of material	Examples of minerals and mining products
CONSTRUCTION	building	building blocks	rocks for building blocks
CONSTRUCTION	building, road making	aggregates	sand, gravel, granite, chippings
CONSTRUCTION	cement, bricks, tiles, plaster	processed materials	limestone, clay, gypsum
METAL WORKING	iron and steel	ferrous metals (contain iron)	iron ores such as haematite, magnetite, limonite
METAL WORKING	smelting for other metals	non-ferrous metals	other metal ores such as bauxite, cassiterite, galena, malachite
FUEL AND POWER	nuclear power	inorganic minerals	pitchblende (uranium ore)
FUEL AND POWER	electricity, domestic heating, gas, industrial furnaces, oil refining	organically formed (from animals and plants)	peat, lignite, coal, anthracite, petroleum (oil), natural gas
CHEMICALS	heavy industry, chemicals, fertilizers, drugs, cosmetics, paints	inorganic minerals	anhydrite, halite, nitrates, potash, sulphur, barytes
CHEMICALS	fertilizers, synthetic fibres, plastics, drugs, cosmetics, paints	organically formed	petroleum (oil), natural gas, coal
PRECIOUS MATERIALS	jewellery, currency	metallic	gold, silver, platinum
PRECIOUS MATERIALS	jewellery, objets d'art	non-metallic	jet, diamonds, other gems such as topaz, garnet, ruby, amethyst
OTHER INDUSTRIES	abrasives, fluxes, ceramics, glass	to make industrial processes	silica, corundum, diamonds, fluorspar, kaolin, felspar
OTHER INDUSTRIES	pottery, glass, salt, cosmetics	consumer products	silica, kaolin, felspar, halite, talc

from the surface directly into the ore body. Mining minerals deeper down, however, may require vertical shafts to be sunk, and then horizontal tunnels to be driven into the ore. Some minerals occur as part of alluvial deposits in streams or lakes and are extracted by dredging. For example, large dredgers scoop up tin-bearing gravels in lakes in Malaysia.

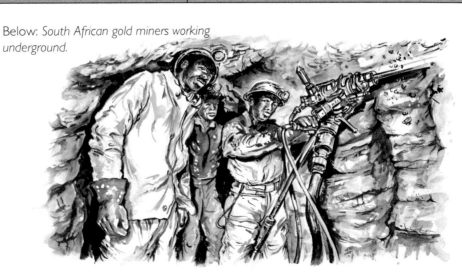

Below: *South African gold miners working underground.*

Coal, Oil and Gas

The fossil fuels, coal, oil and natural gas, are the most important sources of energy in the industrialized world today. The industrial countries, in particular, have become very dependent on them. Yet, though they took millions of years to form, there is a danger that, in the foreseeable future, supplies will run out.

COAL IN BRITAIN

Britain was the first country to build its industrial society on the energy obtained from coal. A century ago, areas like Durham and South Wales each had scores of small collieries from which coal was mined and exported all over the world.

Many of Britain's coal mines have now been closed. This is because the power stations that use the coal have been turning to oil and particularly to gas, which is much cheaper. The mines that remain are mostly larger, newer ones which are highly automated and require few miners. Even imported coal can be cheaper to buy than Britain's own coal.

Coal

Coal is formed from the compacted and deeply buried remains of trees and plants which once grew in swampy forests. Most coals are about 280 million years old. As the dead forests become more compressed, the 'volatile' constituents, such as water and methane, are driven out to leave the carbon behind. The carbon content of coal varies from over 90 per cent (for anthracite) to 70 per cent (bituminous coal) to under 60 per cent (lignite, or brown coal). Anthracite gives off great heat with little flame or smoke, whereas lignite produces lots of smoke but much less heat.

Coal was the basis of the Industrial Revolution in Britain, Germany and the United States. Today these older reserves have largely been worked out, and the world's biggest resources are in China and Russia. There the huge coal bodies are worked in giant open-cast basins, using excavators which can quarry thousands of tonnes a day.

Open-cast coal mining is cheap and efficient, but it is difficult to restore the landscape afterwards.

Oil and natural gas

Oil (petroleum) and natural gas come from microscopic organic remains deposited on the sea-bed and gradually compressed and transformed into oily substances. Oil was first exploited commercially in 1859 but the demand greatly increased with the invention of motor vehicles. Today petroleum is widely used in power stations. It is also the basis of the petrochemical industry, whose many products include fertilizers and plastics.

OIL IN THE MIDDLE EAST

The countries around the Persian Gulf are the world's most important oil-producing area, supplying all the industrialized countries. This has made the oil-producing countries very wealthy, but at the same time has left their economies almost wholly dependent on oil revenues. It is probable that, some time during the next century, their oil resources will run out.

The industrial countries, in particular, have always been concerned that the producers might use oil as a political weapon, by raising prices and perhaps even cutting off their supplies. In 1990 Iraq, an oil-producing country, seized Kuwait, a neighbouring oil-producer. This worried the industrial countries, because it gave Iraq too much control over oil supplies, and led to a war the following year. During the war Iraq tried to use oil to military advantage by releasing oil slicks into the Persian Gulf and burning Kuwait's oil fields. Many people feel that the industrialized countries should look for new forms of energy to reduce their dependence on the Middle Eastern oil-producers.

Right: *Industrialized countries could not function without oil imports.*

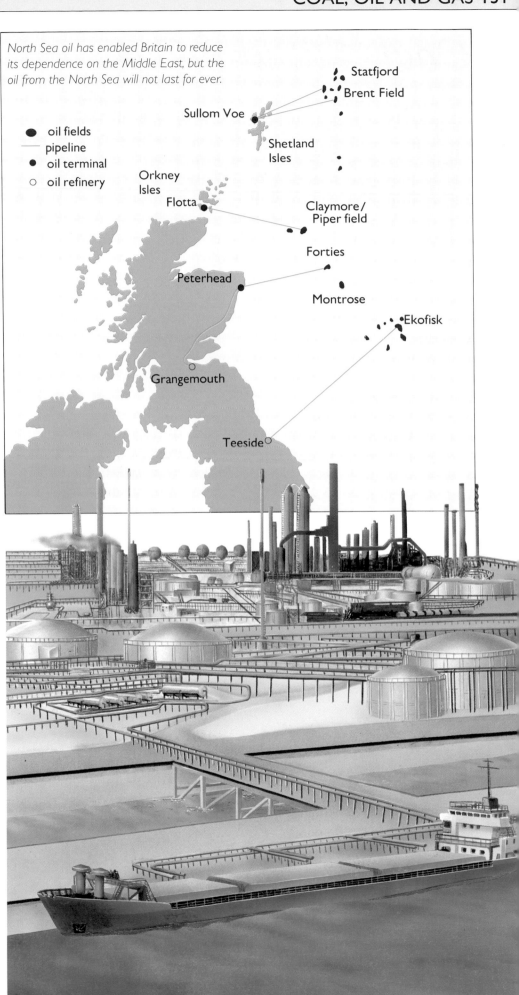

North Sea oil has enabled Britain to reduce its dependence on the Middle East, but the oil from the North Sea will not last for ever.

- ● oil fields
- — pipeline
- ● oil terminal
- ○ oil refinery

Statfjord
Brent Field
Sullom Voe
Shetland Isles
Orkney Isles
Flotta
Claymore/Piper field
Forties
Peterhead
Montrose
Ekofisk
Grangemouth
Teeside

Energy Old and New

For many years people have known that fossil fuels will not last for ever, and that sooner or later new sorts of energy will have to be found. These are of two main kinds: nuclear power, and the so-called 'renewable' sources.

Nuclear power

Nuclear power is electricity generated from nuclear fission, that is, the splitting of the nuclei of uranium atoms to produce energy. Inside a nuclear power station a nuclear reactor produces vast quantities of heat energy which powers turbines and electricity generators, as in an oil-fired or coal-fired power station. Over the past few decades several industrial countries have embarked on nuclear programmes, building nuclear power stations to meet the growing demand for electricity. Britain has 12 such stations producing six per cent of its electricity, compared with 11 per cent nuclear electricity in Japan and 27 per cent in France.

The industry has suffered setbacks, however, and some countries have now cut short their nuclear programmes. Nuclear generated electricity has turned out to be more expensive than expected, and people have become more concerned about safety aspects. A fire in a nuclear reactor at Chernobyl in Ukraine in 1986 led to the contamination of an area 30km (19 miles) wide and made 60,000 buildings unsafe to live in. The effects of the radioactive cloud produced were measurable in Scandinavia, and in western Britain, 2,700km (1,700 miles) away. There are also the problems of where to dispose of the radioactive waste from the reactors, and how to decommission, that is, shut down old power stations once they have reached the end of their working lives.

Renewable resources

The problems with nuclear power have made scientists look much more closely at 'renewable' energy sources, such as the Sun, the sea, water and wind. Some of them, like hydroelectricity (from falling water) and geothermal power (from hot rocks underground),

Britain's nuclear power stations are all outside heavily populated areas. Most are on the coast because they need large quantities of water for cooling.

Dounreay

Torness

Hunterston

Chapelcross

Sellafield

Heysham

Wylfa

Trawsfynydd

Sizewell

Bradwell

Oldbury

Hinkley Point

Dungeness

Winfrith

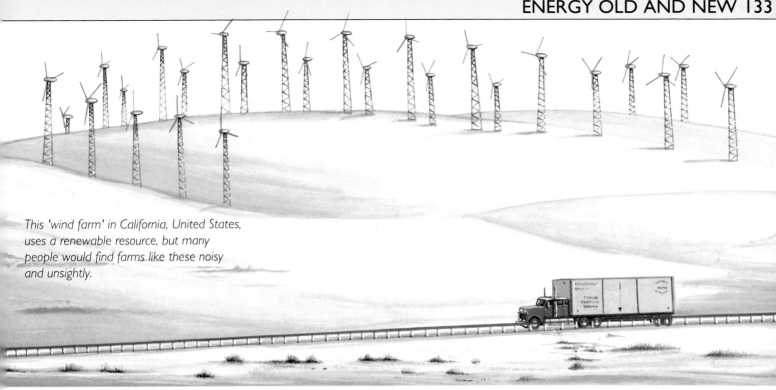

This 'wind farm' in California, United States, uses a renewable resource, but many people would find farms like these noisy and unsightly.

are already well established, but there are not many places in the world where they can be developed on a large scale. Other sources of energy might include wind power, using farms of giant windmills; wave power, harnessing the motion of the sea; solar power, using the Sun to heat solar panels; and tidal power, using the movement of the tides at barrages constructed across estuaries. All these sources have been shown to be technically possible and no more costly than conventional forms of power, but they have yet to be adopted on a large scale worldwide.

In the Third World the energy used by most people comes from renewable resources. In some countries, for example Nepal, Ethiopia and Tanzania, up to 80 per cent of people depend on the wood that they collect for their fuel. However, these countries are now facing an energy crisis as overpopulation and deforestation deplete their fuel wood resources, so that people often have to forage for long distances to find the fuel they need for heat and cooking.

An energy source that poorer countries might develop further is biogas or methane, generated from dung collected together and allowed to rot. It is already used in 46 countries and provides the main source of cooking fuel for many Third World villages.

outlet pit

biogas chamber

inlet

gas outlet

gas storage chamber

fermentation chamber

Left: Biogas chambers use animal and human waste and rotting vegetation to generate methane. The remains can be used as fertilizer. Biogas chambers are relatively cheap to build.

Water for All?

Water does not merely sustain all forms of life; it also plays a large part in keeping the world's economies going. The world uses some 3,000cu. km (700 cubic miles) of water a year, of which only about five per cent is consumed for domestic purposes such as drinking and washing. Of the remainder, 73 per cent is used for irrigation and 22 per cent for industry.

Domestic use

Most of the world's water is used in the developed, industrial countries, where piped supplies are readily available. In New York each person uses around 300 litres (66 gallons) per day. In developing countries water use is much less because water often has to be carried long distances from wells or standpipes, or purchased from water carriers.

Industrial and agricultural use

Without water, industry would grind to a halt. It is used for washing, as a coolant, as a solvent, and to flush out pollutants. Some industries, including the steel, paper and plastics industries, are especially heavy consumers of water. The electricity industry depends on water for power generation as hydroelectricity, and for condensing steam in its giant cooling towers.

Most rural settlements depend on traditional methods of irrigation.

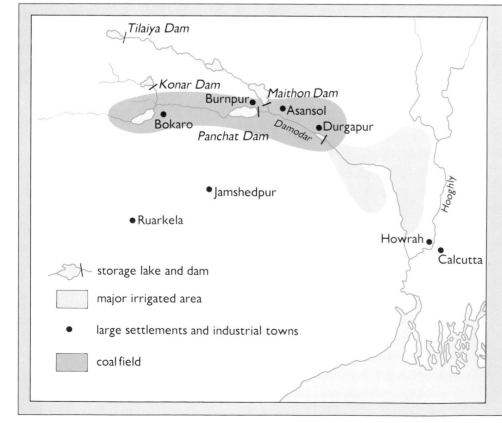

storage lake and dam

major irrigated area

● large settlements and industrial towns

coal field

THE DAMODAR VALLEY SCHEME

In India the Damodar Valley scheme is an example of how water can be used for several purposes at once. A series of five dams has been constructed along the river's length, each dam having a reservoir upstream to store excess water in times of flood. The scheme provides hydroelectric power generated at the dams for industries in the Damodar valley and in the city of Calcutta; control of the Damodar's flow during flood periods; irrigated agriculture on the Ganges–Hooghly flood plain; and water for industries and domestic use.

Although the scheme has produced some environmental problems such as an increase in water-related diseases, it also makes a major contribution to India's economic development.

Water for irrigation is vital to agriculture, as 12 per cent of the world's cultivated land is irrigated, and often crops grown on irrigated land are harvested more than once a year. Sometimes, however, irrigation has led to water resources being overused. For instance, so much water has been taken out of the Aral Sea in Kazakhstan for irrigation that the sea has almost completely dried up. This might even alter the climate of central Asia in the years ahead.

Right: *A comparison of the amount of water used each day by a British city dweller and a villager in Bangladesh.*

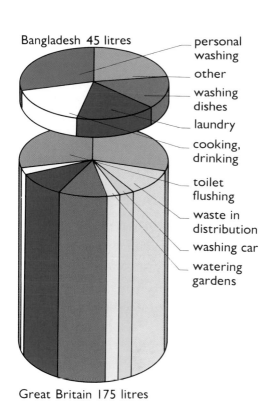

Bangladesh 45 litres

personal washing
other
washing dishes
laundry
cooking, drinking
toilet flushing
waste in distribution
washing car
watering gardens

Great Britain 175 litres

WATER IN THE MIDDLE EAST

Water could be a new source of conflict in the Middle East. The population of the area might grow by as much as 50 per cent over the next 10 years, yet much of the region is desert and there are few perennial (all year) rivers. Persian Gulf countries such as Saudi Arabia and Kuwait already have to obtain some of their water from desalination plants, which are expensive.

Turkey is developing a scheme to build 22 dams on the rivers Tigris and Euphrates for new irrigated land. But this could bring Turkey into conflict with neighbouring Syria and Iraq, who, because they also use the water from these rivers, fear there will soon be less for them. Another dam, on the Yarmuk river, will provide more water for Syria and Jordan but there will be less for Israel, who also uses the Yarmuk. This could be yet a further source of tension between Israel and its Arab neighbours.

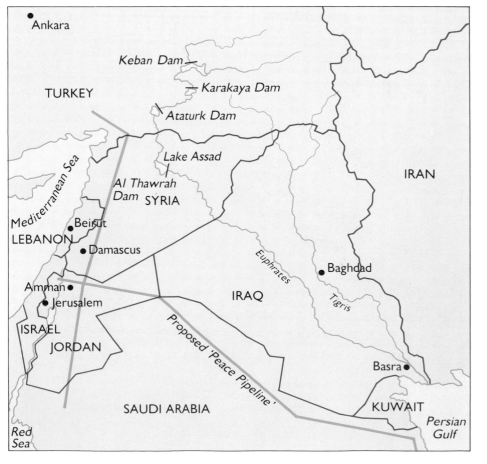

Manufacturing

Manufacturing is a 'secondary' activity – it uses raw materials which it then changes into new products. To do this, it requires labour and machinery, and factories or workshops. Manufacturers also need suppliers of raw materials, a market for their products, and a range of supporting services such as transport and finance.

Light industries on a modern industrial estate.

Types of industry

Heavy industries use heavy, bulky raw materials. The cost of these, together with the cost of transporting them to the factory and the finished product to the market, makes up a large part of the total price of the product. Examples of heavy industries are steelmaking, chemicals and shipbuilding.

Light industries, on the other hand, use lightweight, easily transportable materials. Labour and marketing costs contribute much to the total cost, as in, for example, electrical goods, or goods made from plastics.

A third industrial group, the assembly industries, are concerned with putting together components and items made elsewhere. Car assembly plants, for instance, use many items, few of which may be made at the plant itself. Engines may be made at a different factory, while some specialist components, such as electrical equipment, may be made by other manufacturers.

In developed countries, many industries produce what are known as 'consumer' goods. This means that they are made for direct sale to the public, rather than for sale to businesses or as materials for other industries. The consumer industries depend heavily for their success on advertising, marketing, and the ability to develop new products to keep up with changing fashions and life-styles.

A steelworks, an example of a heavy industry.

Industrial locations

Factories are built in different locations according to their needs. Heavy industries are likely to be found near their source of raw materials in order to minimize transport costs (such as the cement works in the diagram). Some industries are close to the markets they serve, which often means being near a town (for example, the brewery). Industries relying on imported raw materials may locate at ports or other tidewater sites (the oil refinery).

Light industries can usually be found in small factory units on modern industrial or trading estates, close to main roads and motorways for easy distribution of goods. Industries using huge quantities of electricity, such as aluminium smelting, need to be near their power source. The car industry in the picture spreads over a large area and needs a site with plenty of space. Small craft industries, such as hand-made pottery, often choose to be in villages or other rural settings where they can use local skills and sell their products to tourists.

Governments and planners play a part in deciding the location of industries. Some governments may give grants or provide other financial incentives to encourage manufacturers to start businesses in areas of high unemployment. Sometimes planners refuse permission to build factories in rural areas where they might damage the environment.

Different types of industrial locations.

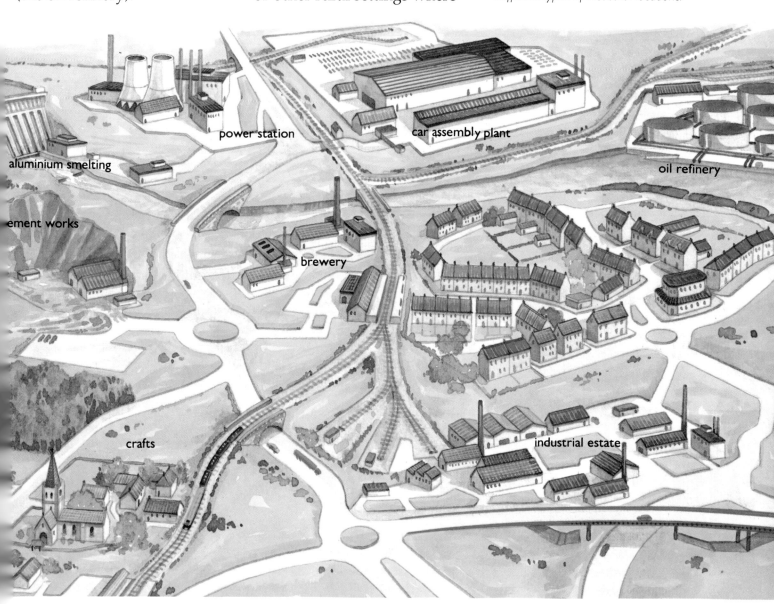

power station

car assembly plant

aluminium smelting

oil refinery

cement works

brewery

crafts

industrial estate

Industries for Tomorrow

Industry worldwide is changing. Recently, a whole new range of industries based on high technology has emerged. Whereas companies have closed and unemployment has risen in many areas associated with the traditional industries, in other places, often with no previous industrial history, new industries have been springing up.

What are 'hi-tec' industries?

High-technology or 'hi-tec' industries include computers, micro-electronics, robotics and other products and services associated with information technology. They are based on the use of the silicon chip – an electronic circuit on a tiny piece of silicon – used to store huge quantities of information at very fast speeds. High technology products also include business machines, video and audio equipment, and the software (tapes and disks) needed to operate them. These new technologies have a vast range of applications, from office computers, to robots in car assembly plants, and to military guided-missile defence systems. Often as much as 25 per cent of the workforce in a 'hi-tec' industry is highly educated, compared with just five per cent for manufacturing industry as a whole.

Some of the products of high technology.

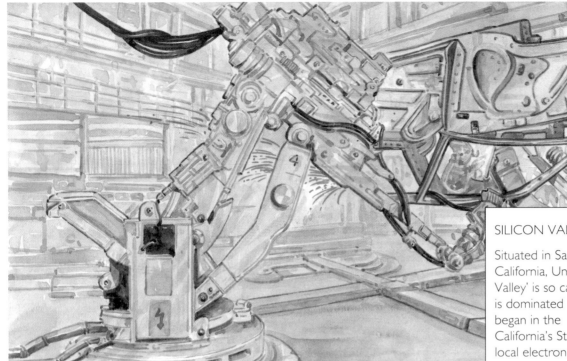

Where are they found?

High technology industries are found in a variety of locations. Some businesses start in a very small way, perhaps with a handful of people in a workshop making specialized electronic components. They often set up business where they can make contact with other firms making similar or complementary products, or where relevant research is being carried out. In this way small clusters of 'hi-tec' establishments grow up in the same area.

However, most high-technology production is in the hands of large multinational corporations with branch plants in many countries. While they may conduct research and development in older industrialized countries such as the United States or Japan, their mass-production factories are usually in the newly industrializing countries of the Far East, such as Singapore, Taiwan or South Korea, where labour is skilled but cheap.

A new dawn?

High-technology industries have sometimes been called 'sunrise' industries, because they were thought to herald a new dawn. At one time, people believed that the 'hi-tec' era would bring everyone less work and more leisure time by replacing human labour with machines. In fact, while the new technology may have contributed to unemployment, it has not necessarily made life easier, and in some ways may have added to the stressful pace of modern living.

Above: The car industry now employs far fewer people. Many of the jobs on the production line are carried out by computerized robots.

SILICON VALLEY

Situated in Santa Clara county in California, United States, 'Silicon Valley' is so called because its industry is dominated by 'hi-tec' products. It began in the 1950s with research by California's Stanford University and by local electronics manufacturers. Through a combination of business initiative, good research facilities and good communications, it grew in size and prestige.

Today Silicon Valley stretches for 80km (50 miles) south-east of San Francisco, with most of the bigger firms sited around Palo Alto and San Jose. Until recently there were plenty of sites for expansion and for new businesses, but the area is now becoming very congested. Some firms have preferred to expand outside the area; one computer company with 20 factories in Silicon Valley has now established branch plants in Texas, Singapore and Ireland.

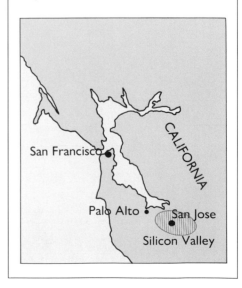

Offices and Services

Supporting the 'primary' and 'secondary' sectors of industry – the provision of raw materials and manufacturing – are the service industries, the so-called 'tertiary' sector. In modern industrial societies the range of services is very complex, and the tertiary sector is a major employer. It is less important in developing countries. In Japan more than half the population works in service industries, compared with less than 20 per cent in India.

Skyscraper office blocks dominate the skyline of most large cities.

Types of services

Many services are in the 'public sector', which means that they are provided by or for national or local government. Other services are in the 'commercial' or 'private' sector. These are run by largely private firms, whose aim is to make a profit for the company. Altogether, services include a wide range of employment: 'blue collar' (manual) work, such as driving buses or trains, or work in shops; 'white collar' (clerical) work, in offices; self-employment (covering everything from highly paid work as a business consultant to low-paid work as a porter or shoe-shiner); and professional, managerial and executive employment, often in financial, legal or administrative services.

Office employment

Office work accounts for a large share of employment in the tertiary sector. Every business generates some paper work, and in larger businesses the offices are separate from the factory or production areas. In town and city centres office buildings for different service industries tend to be found together. They usually include the headquarters of companies, banks and financial services, as well as others that deal directly with the public, such as employment agencies, post offices or estate agents. Many services make use of each other, and benefit by being close together.

In cities and larger towns, the demand for office space

Main groups	Types	Users	Some examples
Public	Utilities	Personal and business	Water, power, gas, waste disposal
	Social	Personal	Education, health, recreation
		Business	Trading estates, training centres
	Administrative	Local government	City hall services, public housing, libraries
		National government	Job centres, training centres
Commercial	Retail and sales	Personal	Shops, department stores
		Business	Wholesale warehouses, storage, maintenance services
	Legal	Personal and business	Solicitors, estate agents, surveyors
	Financial	Personal and business	Banks, insurance, post office, stock exchange
	Leisure	Active	Golf courses, sports clubs, adventure holiday centres
		Passive	Professional football, cinemas, bingo
Transport and communication	Passenger	Personal and business	Rail, air, shipping, road services
	Freight	Personal and business	Rail, air, shipping, road services, post office
	Information	Personal and business	Telephone network, post office

Above: *The 'tertiary' sector includes many different sorts of services.*

An architect's model of a business park, far away from the city centre.

has outgrown the land available in the 'central business district'. This has encouraged office employment to expand upwards rather than outwards. The first skyscraper office blocks were built in the United States a century ago. Since then they have become a familiar feature of city skylines everywhere, often dwarfing the older historic buildings of the city centre.

AN OFFICE PARK IN HAMBURG

In some countries lack of space and high costs in the city centre have caused new office building to move outside to 'green field' sites. In Europe one of the largest 'office parks' is the City-Nord development in Hamburg in Germany. It has an attractive setting in a parkland area on the outskirts of the city, with shops, banks and restaurants close by for office users. It is easily accessible from main roads and from the airport. City-Nord employs about 30,000 office workers. Some planners think that as city centres become more crowded, office parks like City-Nord will increase in number.

References

Agricultural Revolution The changes in farming methods and techniques which began in Europe in the 18th century and gradually spread to other parts of the world. They included the introduction of crop rotation, selective animal breeding and new machinery. In the present century a 'new agricultural revolution' has been based on chemicals and scientific plant breeding.

Aquaculture The cultivation of fish for food, for example fish farming.

Arable farming Farming in which the main activity is the growing of crops.

Assembly industry An industry concerned with the assembly of components made by other manufacturers.

Bush fallowing *See* **Shifting cultivation.**

Business park An area of land set aside for commercial premises; it may include industries, especially of the high-technology type, and offices.

Cash crop A crop grown for sale off the farm, rather than one consumed by the farmer.

Consumer goods Industrial products intended for direct sale to the public rather than as materials for other manufacturers.

Desalination The conversion of sea water into drinking water, by removing the salt content.

Drift A tunnel dug by miners directly into a rock layer or vein.

Evaporite Soluble mineral deposits derived from weathered material. The mineral is washed into lakes and then left behind once the water has evaporated, to form a new sedimentary layer.

Extensive farming Farming of poorer land on a large scale, often giving low yields per unit area but high yields per worker.

Factory farming The rearing of, for example, poultry indoors under controlled conditions to stimulate growth and maximize output.

Fossil fuel A fuel source derived from the remains of plants or animals. Coal, oil (petroleum) and natural gas are fossil fuels.

Green Revolution The spread of modern scientific farming techniques to developing countries.

Heavy industry Industry which uses heavy raw materials or produces heavy, bulky products, all of which are costly to transport.

Industrial estate An area of land set aside for industry. It often includes a range of industrial plants, and many smaller factories.

Intensive farming Farming that utilizes high inputs of capital, energy or labour to achieve high yields per worker and per unit area.

Irrigation The distribution of water to land for growing crops in areas which would otherwise be too dry.

Light industry Industry based on light, easily transportable materials.

Lode A mineral-bearing deposit in the ground.

Multinational company A large company based in one country which also operates in several others.

Multi-purpose project A scheme of development which aims to fulfil several needs at once. An example might be the building of a large dam and reservoir, which could regulate water supply, control floods, provide hydroelectricity, supply irrigation water, and be used for recreation such as boating or water sports.

Newly industrializing country (NIC) A country that has only recently developed its industries or services. Hong Kong, Taiwan, South Korea and Singapore are examples.

Office park An area set aside specifically for office development. Office parks are usually in open locations with landscaped surroundings, and close to major road links.

Open-cast mining A form of mining in which minerals are extracted by excavator from directly below the surface.

Ore A mineral body containing metal. The ore has to be refined or purified in order for the metal to be extracted.

Pastoral farming Farming in which the main activity is the rearing of livestock. It includes commercial ranching and nomadic herding.

Polder An area of land reclaimed from the sea in the Netherlands.

Primary activity Economic activity or livelihood which makes direct use of the Earth's natural resources, eg hunting, fishing, forestry, mining and agriculture.

Public sector The parts of the economy controlled by national or local government. They include the civil service and most health and education services.

Renewable resource A resource which is renewed by natural means. Wave, wind, solar and tidal power are examples of renewable energy resources. Others are hydroelectricity, geothermal energy and energy from fuelwood.

Secondary activity The conversion of 'primary' raw materials into manufactured goods.

Shifting cultivation A kind of farming in which both the cultivated area and the settlement move from time to time around an area of forest.

Subsistence farming The production of food and raw materials for use by the farmer and his family, but not for sale.

Sunrise industry An industry based on high technology, particularly one involving computers, microelectronics or information technology.

Tertiary activity Employment in the provision of services.

Vicious cycle A phase of increasing hardship and poverty in which conditions gradually get worse.

Leisure, Travel and Trade

Holidays and Tourism

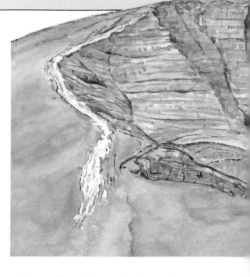

A century ago only wealthier people could afford the time or the money to go on holiday, whereas today holidaymaking is a normal part of life for many people. Service industries have developed to provide for leisure needs; these include package holidays, charter airlines, coach firms, hotels and catering, gift shops and entertainment centres. The tourist industry is a growing business in all countries.

The industrialized world

Holidays and tourism have grown fastest in the industrialized countries. Compared with half a century ago, people have a shorter working week, longer holidays, and more money to spend on leisure. Many more people now own cars, which give them access to almost anywhere at any time they wish.

Greater leisure for everyone brings its own problems. People and their vehicles concentrate at scenic places along the coast or in the countryside, or at places offering leisure facilities and entertainments. The concentrations are most marked at weekends, at peak holiday times, and throughout the summer. Long traffic queues and tailbacks become common along well used holiday routes, for example to the south-west of England, or to the south of France.

Many more people now take holidays abroad. Fifty or sixty years ago a week at the seaside was the most common form of holiday. About thirty years ago, holidays in neighbouring countries became more common. Now some people can afford holidays in more distant parts of the world – for instance in Africa or the Caribbean.

Above: *Some footpaths in scenic areas are being eroded by too many visitors.*

Below: *Glossy brochures invite people to spend their holidays in distant countries.*

The developing world

In the developing world the leisure position is very different, since far fewer people can afford holidays or have much leisure time. The low wages people earn in the cities of developing countries are hardly enough to buy food, or pay rent. In the countryside long hours are spent growing the crops needed to survive. Only the wealthy can afford to go on holiday.

Nevertheless tourism is becoming more important in developing countries to cater for tourists from abroad. European and American visitors are attracted to tropical countries because of the warm, sunny climate, the unspoilt scenery, and the opportunity to see a different culture. Many poorer countries have come to see the importance of the money foreign visitors spend, especially in creating jobs.

Some countries have developed their tourist potential much more than others. Jamaica and Barbados receive twice as much money from foreign visitors as their own people spend abroad. Some developing countries have deliberately tried to plan for tourist growth by building facilities, services and resorts. In Kenya large areas of bush savanna have been turned over to safari parks.

TOURISM IN THE SEYCHELLES

The Seychelles in the Indian Ocean are a group of 100 tiny islands spread across 400,000sq. km (over 150,000 square miles) of tropical sea. The warm, sunny weather all the year round, white sandy beaches, and beautiful coral reefs attract increasing numbers of visitors. The first modern hotel was opened in 1972, and today the Seychelles receive over 100,000 visitors a year.

Tourism accounts for about 35 per cent of the government income of the Seychelles. But the industry is very vulnerable to changes in the world economy, and numbers of visitors fell sharply during the world recession of the early 1980s.

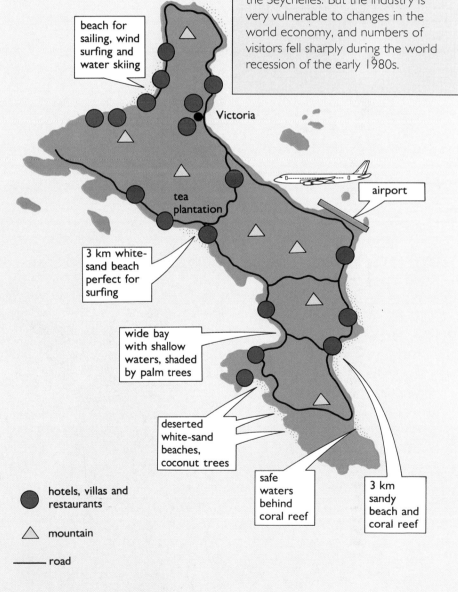

beach for sailing, wind surfing and water skiing

Victoria

tea plantation

airport

3 km white-sand beach perfect for surfing

wide bay with shallow waters, shaded by palm trees

deserted white-sand beaches, coconut trees

safe waters behind coral reef

3 km sandy beach and coral reef

● hotels, villas and restaurants

△ mountain

——— road

Some of the tourist attractions of the island of Mahe in the Seychelles.

National and Wildlife Parks

The growth of tourism has led many countries to set aside areas of countryside or coastline and designate them as 'National Parks'. How these are organized differs from country to country, but their common purpose is to promote greater use of the recreational facilities they provide, while conserving the character of the landscape and scenery.

National Parks in England and Wales

There are 11 National Parks in England and Wales, including, most recently, the Norfolk Broads. Many of these are not only tourist areas, but also tracts of working countryside where people make a living from farming, forestry, quarrying or water supply. Any proposals for new developments are scrutinized by planning boards who are keen to prevent industry from spoiling the landscape or damaging the environment.

THE PEAK DISTRICT NATIONAL PARK

The Peak District National Park in England covers 1,400sq. km (about 540 square miles), mostly of high open moorland. The Park contains important stately homes and spectacular limestone caves. It lies close to the conurbations of Greater Manchester and South Yorkshire, from where most of the visitors come. More than 22 million cars cross the Park boundary annually, and on a fine Sunday in summer there may be 100,000 visitors.

The large number of people causes problems for the Park authorities, who sometimes have to turn day-trippers away from overloaded sites and close heavily congested roads.

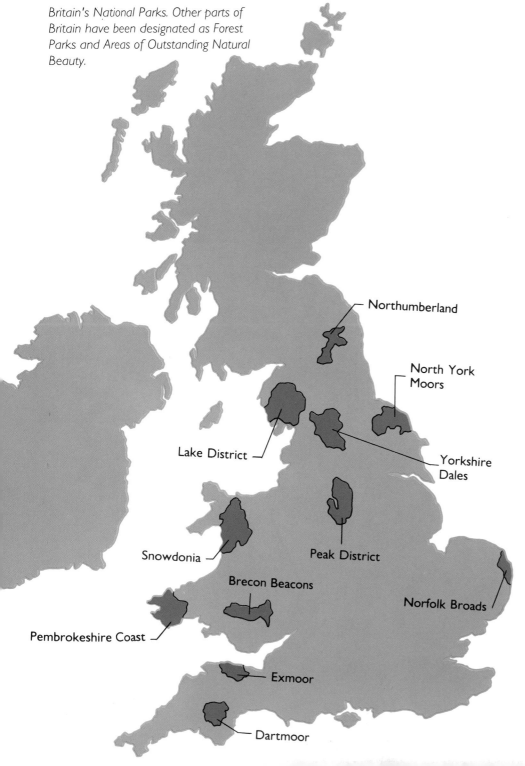

Britain's National Parks. Other parts of Britain have been designated as Forest Parks and Areas of Outstanding Natural Beauty.

Northumberland

North York Moors

Lake District

Yorkshire Dales

Snowdonia

Peak District

Brecon Beacons

Norfolk Broads

Pembrokeshire Coast

Exmoor

Dartmoor

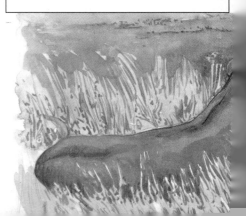

AYERS ROCK, AUSTRALIA

One of Australia's most famous landmarks and tourist sites is Ayers Rock in the deserts of the Northern Territory. The rock has a spectacular setting, giving breathtaking views of the surrounding desert landscape.

The government of Northern Territory has tried to promote Ayers Rock as a tourist site, while still preserving its 'wilderness' character. The surrounding area has been made into the Uluru National Park, now reached by a new highway and airport. Inside the Park the newly-built Yulara holiday resort provides camping, a visitor information office, and an Aboriginal craft centre. New link roads control access to the Rock. The scheme has been planned to cater for 6,000 visitors a day without damage to the natural environment.

Wildlife parks

Kenya and Tanzania have tried to develop tourism, and at the same time conserve their game resources, through wildlife parks. These are huge areas of open plains and savannas, such as the Serengeti National Park, which covers 15,000 sq. km (nearly 6,000 square miles), about half the size of Belgium. The parks enable large mammals such as elephants to be protected from poachers and to be viewed or studied by visitors on organized 'safari' trips guided by park rangers. In this way the number of visitors to the parks is carefully controlled.

Left: Wildlife parks serve to protect wild animals of African countries and make it easier for tourists to see them.

Inland and Water Transport

In the industrial world transport is mostly mechanized, but in the Third World it often depends on humans and animals for its motive power. One of the oldest ways of moving people and goods – water transport – still plays a vital role in many parts of the world today.

Mechanized and non-mechanized transport

In the Middle East camels are still used to carry both people and goods, and in much of Asia ox-carts are still in service. Bicycles are a major form of urban transport in countries such as China and Vietnam. Many journeys for which motorized transport would be used in the developed countries are often made on foot in the Third World. Non-motorized transport is not only cheaper – in that it does not depend on oil or costly machinery – it is sometimes more suited to the conditions. In Greece, for example, donkeys are used to climb steep mountain tracks that would be inaccessible to motor vehicles.

Inland waterways

The Grand Canal in China, which is still in use today, is the world's oldest inland waterway. It was begun as long ago as the 5th century BC. Very much later, in the 18th century, Britain, under the impact of the early Industrial Revolution, developed one of the first canal networks, to move freight between the new industrial centres. Nowadays, most of Britain's inland freight is moved by road or rail, because it is quicker, and the canals are used mainly for recreation.

In mainland Europe, however, the canals and navigable rivers are put to much greater use. One of the most important of these waterways is the River Rhine, which passes through four countries. It is now being linked with the Danube by a scheme using the River Main, in Germany, where inland shipping accounts for 25 per cent of the freight carried.

Ocean shipping

Ocean shipping has changed considerably over the past 30 or 40 years. Passenger liners have now disappeared apart from luxury cruisers, and there are fewer general cargo ships. Instead there are more specialized types of vessel, such as oil tankers, container ships and bulk grain carriers. Ships have also become bigger, with some oil tankers now exceeding 500,000 tonnes dead-weight, about 10 times bigger than tankers of half a century ago.

Larger vessels can present their own problems, in that they are often unable to find ports with water deep enough to handle them. Large oil tankers (called supertankers)

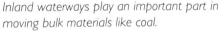

Inland waterways play an important part in moving bulk materials like coal.

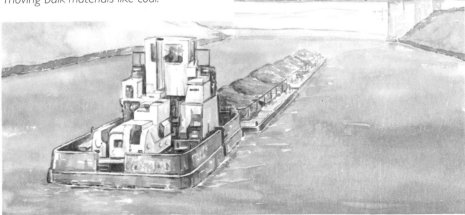

THE PANAMA CANAL

The Panama Canal, which was opened in 1914, links the Pacific and Atlantic Oceans. For sea journeys between eastern and western United States it saves up to 13,000km (8,100 miles) of sailing around Cape Horn. However, deforestation is causing soil erosion and the silting up of the reservoirs which supply the canal, so that there is now less water to replenish it. In the future it may have to close during dry parts of the year.

also pose risks of disastrous pollution if they run aground – as happened when the *Exxon Valdez* ran aground off the coast of Alaska in 1989.

Some quite short waterways are of immense importance to world shipping as a whole. Among them are the Suez Canal and the Strait of Hormuz, which carries two-thirds of the industrial world's supply of oil. The industrial countries sent their navies to protect the Strait during the Iran–Iraq war of the 1980s and the Gulf War of 1991.

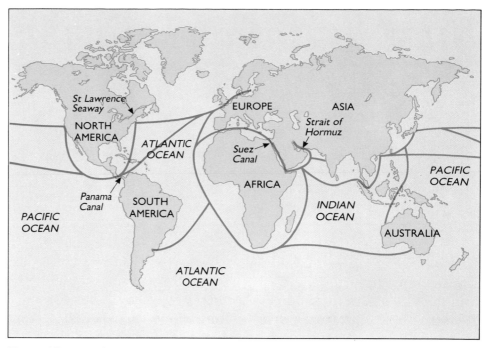

The world's main shipping routes.

PIPELINES

Pipelines have become important in the present century for transporting water, oil, natural gas and some solids that can be made into a slurry (a semi-liquid mixture). Russia is one of the world's leading builders of pipelines. Russian pipelines carry oil and natural gas from oil fields to its industrial regions and to countries in eastern Europe. One pipeline, which serves Poland, eastern Germany and Czechoslovakia, is 5,327km (3,329 miles) long.

Types of ships and harbour facilities. Not all of them would be found at any one port.

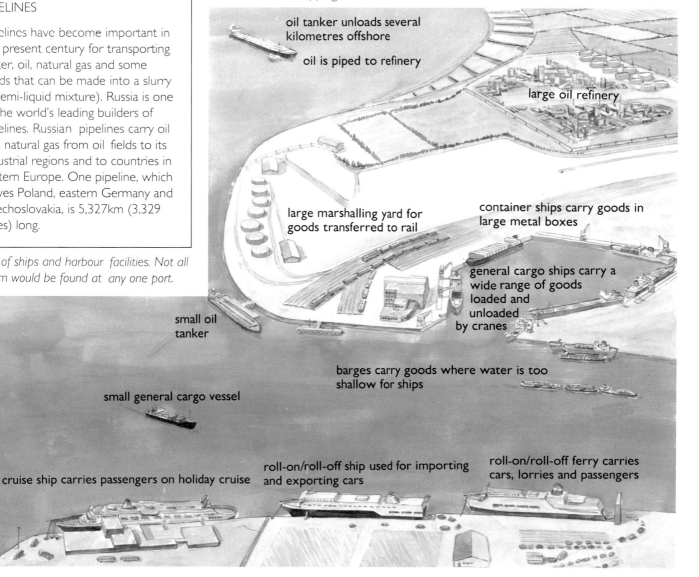

oil tanker unloads several kilometres offshore

oil is piped to refinery

large oil refinery

large marshalling yard for goods transferred to rail

container ships carry goods in large metal boxes

general cargo ships carry a wide range of goods loaded and unloaded by cranes

small oil tanker

barges carry goods where water is too shallow for ships

small general cargo vessel

cruise ship carries passengers on holiday cruise

roll-on/roll-off ship used for importing and exporting cars

roll-on/roll-off ferry carries cars, lorries and passengers

Road and Rail Transport

In the 19th century the railways revolutionized transport, gradually spreading from the industrialized countries across the world. They helped to open up new lands such as North America and Australia, by providing a communications network. In the present century railways have been in decline in many countries, as more and more people have taken to the roads in privately owned vehicles.

Railways

The decline of the railways has been most marked in the industrialized countries. Today, in Britain, for example, 20 times more passengers and 10 times more goods by weight are carried by road than by rail. Even Canada, a country whose railways were built to unify the nation, has taken steps to dismantle its national railway network.

Nevertheless there are signs that rail travel may experience a revival in the decades to come. To ease bad traffic congestion on the roads, many major cities, such as Hong Kong, have invested heavily in new rapid-transit systems for taking commuters into and out of city centres. Inter-city travel too, in countries like Japan and France, where there are high-speed rail networks, can also be quicker by rail than by road. The French high-speed trains, the TGVs, can run at up to 300km/h (nearly 190mph).

Transporting large consignments of heavy freight, such as coal in bulk, is also easier by rail, since trains can carry much bigger loads than lorries. However, some developing countries such as Chile do not have a good railway system and therefore most of their freight is moved by road.

Roads

Roads have an advantage over railways, in being able to provide door-to-door transport. From the 1920s, and in particular since the Second World War, car ownership has

Below: *The French TGV (train à grande vitesse) now provides the world's fastest passenger services.*

THE CHANNEL TUNNEL

The Channel Tunnel runs from the south-east coast of England, under the English Channel, to the northern coast of France. It is the first-ever fixed link built between Britain and the European mainland, and one of the major transport projects of the 1990s.

Shuttle trains carrying cars and lorries take only 35 minutes to cross between the British and French terminals. Freight trains from Scotland and northern England save 36 hours on journeys to Belgium and 48 hours on journeys to Germany. This is because they are able to run direct, without having to trans-ship goods from rail to ferry and back to rail again. Passenger trains from London to Paris take less than 3.5 hours, compared with nearly 7 hours by existing train and ferry services. The Channel Tunnel is a valuable contribution to the development of a new high-speed rail network throughout Europe.

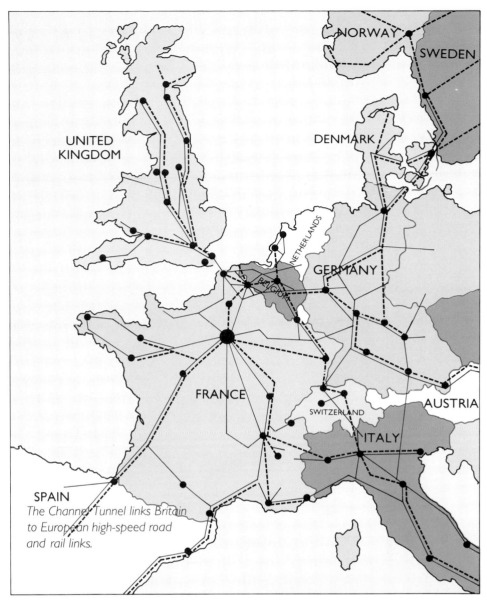

The Channel Tunnel links Britain to European high-speed road and rail links.

expanded enormously, and with it the road network, giving people a choice of when to travel and what route to take. The greatest growth has been in the use of motorways, as they are known in Britain, or 'superhighways' in the United States. During the 1980s motorway traffic in Britain grew at 17 per cent per year compared with 3 per cent for other major roads. But Britain's motorways have become so popular that they are now frequently congested. The M25, encircling London, and opened in 1986, carries far more traffic than expected, and 'tailbacks' several miles long are commonplace.

Below: Commuters are often delayed for long periods in traffic jams on crowded motorways.

Airways and Telecommunications

Today flying is the principal mode of long-distance travel. Journeys that were once made by sea and took several days can now be accomplished by air in a matter of hours. In North America aircraft have almost replaced trains for travel across the continent. As a result, places that are far apart seem much closer together. Satellites have also contributed to 'making the world smaller' by offering news and information services globally at the touch of a button.

World airways

Unlike other forms of transport – road, rail and water – air travel is not confined to the Earth's surface. It is, however, restricted in a number of other ways. For safety reasons, especially on heavily used routes, aircraft are directed along carefully marked air corridors, and their schedules for landing and taking off are tightly controlled. Aircraft also need runways and ground facilities, and this requires them to fly directly between one airport and another, and to keep the number of intermediate stops to a minimum.

Most air traffic is between large cities, with airports serving wide, densely populated areas. Some of the world's busiest air routes are between the cities on the east and west coasts of the United States, and between US and European cities. As well as the regular scheduled airline services, there are also 'charter' travel airlines, which are used

Air travel has now largely replaced ocean shipping and trains for long-distance journeys.

by package-holiday firms to fly their customers to their holiday destinations. In the summer, holiday flights make the airspace over major cities very busy indeed.

Aircraft can handle only small amounts of international freight in terms of total tonnage, and air freight is expensive. They are mainly used for carrying lighter, higher value goods, or perishable goods that need to reach their destination quickly.

Airports

Airports are expensive to build and maintain, and require a huge volume of air-passenger traffic to make them profitable.

The main airports, which are all located close to major population centres, handle many millions of passengers each year. To deal with such a volume of through traffic, the airports need to be well connected to other parts of the country as a whole by fast road and rail routes. With air traffic increasing rapidly, many major world airports are now unable to cope with the volume. London already has two airports at Heathrow and Gatwick, and a third one at Stansted is being developed to meet the rising demand. Some provincial airports in Britain, such as Birmingham and Manchester, have benefited from the increased demand by accepting some of the traffic which the bigger airports are unable to handle.

Telecommunications

Even more than air travel, the modern development of telecommunications has transformed our world into

what has been called a 'global village'. Recent hi-tec developments in the areas of space satellites, optic fibres, microelectronics, lasers and computers have made it possible to beam information across the world at fantastic speeds, and for that information to be processed, analysed, and acted upon within minutes. Many people think that these developments will change our civilization as much as the Industrial Revolution did for earlier generations.

Since 1957 over 14,000 satellites have been launched, of which around 300 are still active. They help with weather forecasting; survey the Earth's surface in detail; provide military information; enable instant television reporting from all parts of the globe; and carry television programmes. Satellites enabled Indonesia to link all its 3,000 islands to its national radio and telephone services.

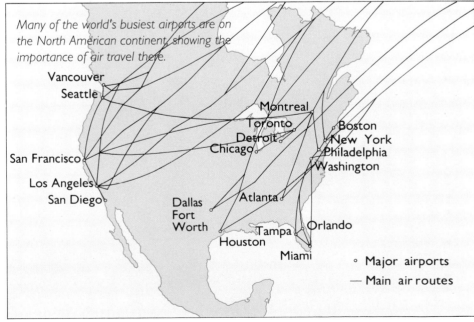

Many of the world's busiest airports are on the North American continent, showing the importance of air travel there.

Vancouver
Seattle
Montreal
Toronto
Detroit
Boston
New York
Chicago
Philadelphia
Washington
San Francisco
Los Angeles
San Diego
Dallas
Fort
Worth
Atlanta
Houston
Tampa
Orlando
Miami

∘ Major airports
— Main air routes

Trade

Trade is essential for all societies. In its simplest form it links different activities which depend on each other, and allows particular places or peoples to specialize in certain products which they can sell or exchange for other things they cannot produce. In the modern world countries are becoming more dependent than ever on their trade with other nations.

Patterns of trade

The most important trade-flows on the global scale take place between the more industrialized 'northern' nations and the less industrialized 'southern' ones. The 'South' produces most of the raw material commodities that go into world trade – especially food and minerals – while the 'North' converts the

Below: *The trade patterns of India, a developing country, and Japan, an industrialized one. Both countries are heavily dependent on imports of petroleum. Japan is much more important as a world trading nation than India.*

raw materials into manufactured goods, many of which are sold back to the 'South' as exports. However the industrialized countries have the financial power to set both the prices they pay for their raw materials, and the prices they charge for their manufactured goods. The result is that the southern countries have been getting steadily poorer compared with the northern ones.

Some poorer countries remain dependent on the export of one commodity – for example, Ethiopia is very

dependent on its coffee exports. This makes such countries very vulnerable to fluctuations in the world price of their staple commodity. Bolivia, for instance, suffered badly in the 1980s because of the collapse of world tin prices.

World trade

Many economists and world leaders agree that this pattern of trade is not good for the long-term future of the world, but disagree on what should be done about it. Some people think that governments should get together to work out a fairer trading system; others think that 'market forces' will sort out the problem on their own; while yet others consider that the 'South' should develop its own internal trading system, free from the influence of the 'North'.

World trading blocs

Some countries with common trading interests have come

INDIA

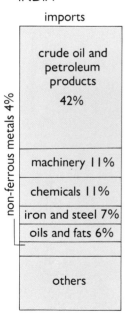

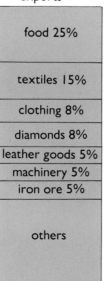

JAPAN

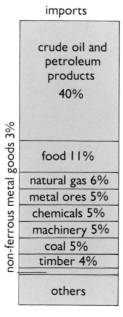

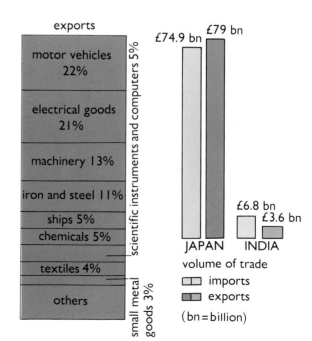

volume of trade
imports
exports
(bn = billion)

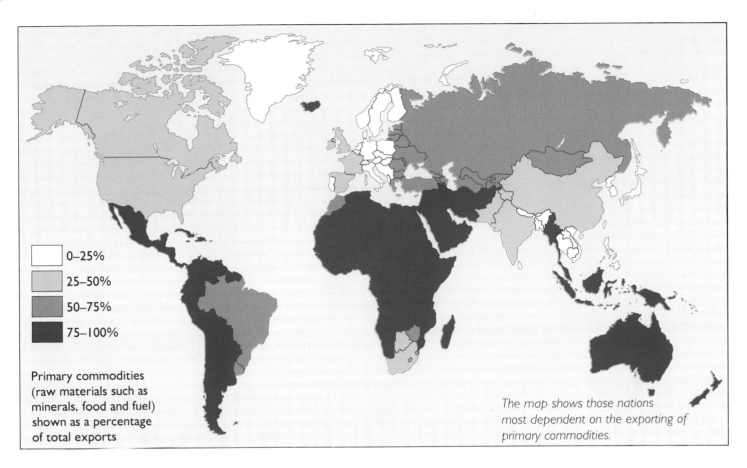

0–25%
25–50%
50–75%
75–100%

Primary commodities
(raw materials such as
minerals, food and fuel)
shown as a percentage
of total exports

*The map shows those nations
most dependent on the exporting of
primary commodities.*

together to form groups or 'blocs' for their mutual benefit. The Organization of Petroleum Exporting Countries (OPEC), is made up of the major oil-producing countries, and its aim is to control the price of oil on the world market. The Latin American Integration Association (LAIA) encourages free trade between its member states, which include most Central and South American countries.

The most powerful international trading association in the near future is likely to be the European Community (EC). Its twelve member states include some of the world's wealthiest countries, which since 1992 have functioned as a 'single market', which means that there are no tariff barriers between the member countries, and there is free movement of capital and labour. In a few years there may be a single European currency. Some people see these developments as steps towards a single European state, but others believe that European political union is still a long way off.

International financial markets such as the London Stock Exchange control world commodity prices.

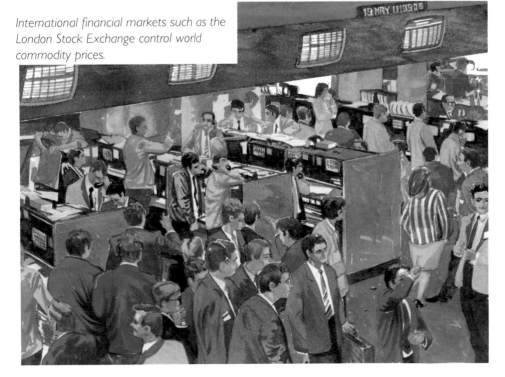

References

Air corridor A route used by aircraft. Highly skilled air-traffic controllers limit the number of aircraft using a corridor at any one time.

Balance of trade The difference between what a country earns for the goods and services it exports, and what it has to pay for those which it imports.

Bulk carrier A ship designed to carry a specific cargo in bulk form. Grain, metal ores and coal are usually shipped on bulk carrier ships.

Charter aircraft An aircraft hired by a group of people or company for a particular flight, especially to a holiday destination.

Common market A grouping of countries into a single market for the goods they all produce. They have a common trade policy which lowers **Tariffs** between them and helps goods to move more cheaply. An example is the European Community.

Commuting The journey to and from work, especially by bus, train or car.

Container ship A cargo ship designed solely to carry large containers. Containers are stacked in a regular pattern, thus maximizing space. Container ships require specialized handling facilities.

Country park A countryside recreation area which provides open space and casual leisure facilities. Country parks are often sited within easy access of built-up areas around large towns or cities.

Entrepôt A port at the focus of many trading routes, often where **Trans-shipment** takes place.

Game park An area set aside for the conservation of wildlife. *See* **Wildlife park.**

Honeypot A beauty spot or otherwise attractive location that receives very large numbers of tourists.

Juggernaut A large, heavy lorry. Most juggernauts are articulated (jointed).

Motorway A road of several lanes built for fast traffic movements. Motorways allow access and exit only at certain points, and no stopping is allowed except in an emergency. Motorways have different names in different countries, for example *autoroute* (France), *autobahn* (Germany) and *autostrada* (Italy).

National Park An area set aside for the conservation of scenery, environment, wildlife, etc, and its enjoyment by visitors. National Parks vary in size from a few hundred to several thousand square kilometres, and their aims and organization vary from country to country.

Node A main place on a transport network. Nodal places are usually centres of industry and population, or places where several routes meet.

Package holiday A holiday in which all arrangements for travel and accommodation are made by the travel company, and are covered by the inclusive price.

Rapid transit A public transport scheme for moving large numbers of commuters into and out of cities, for example an underground railway system.

Resort A town, usually on the coast, where the principal livelihoods of the inhabitants are based on tourism.

Sea lane A fixed ocean route used by shipping. Some sea lanes are very heavily congested, for example the English Channel between Great Britain and France.

Second home A home whose owner lives elsewhere most of the time, so that the second home is only used for leisure at holidays and weekends. Second homes are especially popular in North America and Scandinavia.

Ship canal A canal deep and wide enough to take ocean-going vessels, for example the Suez Canal.

Staple commodity A commodity (raw material etc) on which a country is heavily dependent for its exports.

Tailback A long queue of vehicles on a main road. Tailbacks can result from traffic congestion, accidents, poor weather conditions, etc.

Tariff A duty charged by a country on goods or commodities it imports from other countries. The purpose is to protect the 'home' industry from competition from abroad.

TGV (*Train à grande vitesse*) A high-speed train in France. Other high-speed trains include the 'bullet' trains of Japan.

Tourism The business of providing travel, services etc for holiday travellers. Tourism is a very important part of many economies.

Trading bloc A group of countries between which trading barriers have been eased. *See* **Common market.**

Transport network A system of interconnecting routes, providing ready access from any one place to others on the network, for example a railway system.

Trans-shipment The transfer of cargo from one type of transport to another, for example ship to rail. Trans-shipment is also the transfer of cargo from large ocean-going ships to smaller ones able to use inland waterways.

Wilderness An area largely in its natural, wild state, unspoilt by human activity, in the form of building development, farming etc.

Wildlife park A type of National Park in which the emphasis is on the conservation, study and enjoyment of wildlife rather than scenery.

Index

Page references to illustrations are shown in *italic* type.